Praise for this book...

'This book makes a useful contribution to the rapidly expanding literature on value chains by clarifying the myriad methods, some old, some new, used to finance actors in agricultural value chains.'

Richard L. Meyer, Professor Emeritus, Ohio State University

'I recommend the publication to be read by all stakeholders in the agriculture sector.'

N.V. Ramana, former CEO, BASIX, India and Chairman,
Indian Society of Agribusiness Professionals, India

'This is a "must read" for anyone interested in value chain finance. The authors have moved forward our understanding by presenting a conceptual framework, supported by an extensive use of case studies, which makes this book indispensible for those involved in financing as well as policy makers.'

Kenneth Shwedel, Agricultural Economist

'An insightful and complete analysis of agricultural value chain financing. An essential reference for anyone interested in improving access to agricultural credit in developing countries.'

Mark D. Wenner, Inter-American Development Bank

Agricultural Value Chain Finance
Tools and Lessons

Calvin Miller
and
Linda Jones

Published by
The Food and Agriculture Organization of the United Nations
and
Practical Action Publishing
2010

Practical Action Publishing Ltd
Schumacher Centre for Technology and Development
Bourton on Dunsmore, Rugby,
Warwickshire, CV23 9QZ, UK
www.practicalactionpublishing.org

© FAO, 2010

ISBN 978 1 85339 702 8
FAO ISBN 978 925 106277 7

A catalogue record for this book is available from the British Library.

The authors have asserted their rights under the Copyright Designs and Patents Act
1988 to be identified as authors of this work.

Since 1974, Practical Action Publishing (formerly Intermediate Technology
Publications and ITDG Publishing) has published and disseminated books and
information in support of international development work throughout the world.
Practical Action Publishing is a trading name of Practical Action Publishing Ltd
(Company Reg. No. 1159018), the wholly owned publishing company of Practical
Action. Practical Action Publishing trades only in support of its parent charity
objectives and any profits are covenanted back to Practical Action (Charity Reg. No.
247257, Group VAT Registration No. 880 9924 76).

Cover photo: Potato conveyor belt © FAO/Olivier Thuillier, and authors' own photos
Cover design by Practical Action Publishing
Indexed by Andrea Palmer
Typeset by S.J.I. Services, New Delhi
Printed by Hobbs the Printers Ltd, Totton, Hampshire

Contents

Boxes

Figures

Tables

About the authors

Calvin Miller is an agricultural economist, with a specialization in rural finance. He is Senior Officer and leader of the Agribusiness and Finance Group in the Food and Agriculture Organization of the UN. During his career he has worked in agriculture and financial development in more than 50 countries, with 15 years of global experience in technical assistance, project management and research in rural and agricultural development finance and marketing. He gained direct field experience working for 16 years in Latin America in agricultural and rural finance, agricultural value chain development and agro-enterprise development.

He is also the founder of MicroVest, a private sector social investment fund for microfinance, and a co-founder of the Rural Finance Learning Centre, a multi-institutional resource centre managed by FAO. He has published manuals and other documents on agricultural finance and value chain finance.

Linda Jones is an international consultant specializing in inclusive market development and a technical adviser for sub-sector/value chain development programmes, particularly in agriculture. She has hands-on project management and consulting experience in Eastern Europe, Middle East, Africa and Asia. Linda is a recognized contributor to best practice and advancement of the field of enterprise development, and is a member of the Editorial Committee of *Enterprise Development and Microfinance* journal.

Linda was formerly Chair of the SEEP Board of Directors, the founding Chair of WAM (Women Advancing Microfinance) Canada, and Technical Director of MEDA . She has been a trainer for the Microenterprise Development Institute and ILO for many years, and has published widely on enterprise development, value chain analysis and development, and agricultural value chains.

Acknowledgements

The concept of Value Chain Finance is broad, and the term is used to describe varying aspects of the approach and its supporting tools. Therefore, a nuanced understanding of value chain finance is best derived from the learning of many who are experts in one or multiple aspects of financing the value chain. This volume brings together the experience of many such experts.

This collection is built upon the expertise and contributions of a multitude of persons and their institutions and businesses. It is not always feasible to provide footnotes and references to all these people and their presentations, papers, discussions and other contributions. The presentations and papers can be accessed on the Rural Finance Learning Centre (RFLC) at www.ruralfinance.org/id/48273 and publications at www.ruralfinance.org/id/1813. The authors appreciate this valuable information and the rich insights, which can now be shared with a wider audience. The volume also draws from two articles by one of the authors published in the *Enterprise Development and Microfinance* journal, Vol. 13, Nos. 2 and 3 and Vol. 19, No. 4.

The authors are extremely grateful for the input of nearly 90 papers and/or presentations made by experts and practitioners in this field from around the world. In particular, the authors would like to acknowledge the persons who made valuable written contributions through publications or summary documents from international conferences organized by the FAO on this topic. These include: Rodolfo Quirós and Claudio Gonzalez-Vega in Latin America, Yogesh Ghore in Asia, Mumbi Kimathi and Jonathan Campaigne in Africa, Larry Digal in Southeast Asia and Michael Winn in Eastern Europe. The case studies in the text have been graciously drafted by Grace Ruto, Farm Concern; Jonathan Campaign, DrumNet; Kalyan Chakravarthy and Raju Poosapati, YES Bank; Enrique Zamorra, LAFISE; and Emmanuelle LeCourtois and Äke Olofsson, FAO.

In addition the authors would like to note the insightful contributions made by Richard Meyer, Anita Campion and Mark Wenner in providing their expert review comments.

Finally, strong recognition is given to the FAO for its support for the international conferences on the topic and allocation of the time and resources needed for developing this volume. Special thanks also goes to the colleagues in the FAO who contributed research and review to the publication, including Doyle Baker, Prasun Das, Eva Gálvez-Nogales, Ivana Gegenbauer, Martin Hilmi, Maria Pagura, Carlos da Silva, Andrew Shepherd, and Tigist Woldetsadik.

Preface

This volume provides a global review of experiences and learning on the broad subject of value chain finance for agriculture in developing countries. Value chains in agriculture comprise a set of actors who conduct a linked sequence of value-adding activities involved in bringing a product from its raw material stage to the final consumer. Value chain finance, as described in this volume, refers to the financial flows to those actors from both within the value chain and financial flows to those actors from the outside as a result of their being linked within a value chain.

The purpose of this book is to provide an understanding of the emerging field of agricultural value chain finance. Key questions include:

- What is value chain finance, how is it applied and what can it offer to strengthen agricultural development?
- How can financial systems, governments and services be prepared for the demands of financing modern agri-food chains?
- How does agricultural value chain financing affect inclusion, especially for small producers and what can be done to make these systems more inclusive?
- What can governmental and non-governmental (NGO) agencies do to support increased and more effective agricultural financing through value chains?

These issues are addressed through examination of a wide array of experiences and illustrations of large and small organizations from around the world that are participating in or linked to agricultural value chain financing. The central concern of the volume is not to take a stand on the virtues and weaknesses of value chain finance, but rather to describe how the various types of value chains are being used to strengthen and extend financial products and services to the agricultural sector. Many of the value chain finance instruments and processes are not new; however, what is new and noteworthy is the extent to which value chain finance is being utilized by financial institutions, agribusinesses and farmers. Noteworthy are the variations across applications, the range of organizations that are facilitating value chain finance in innovative ways, the emergence of integrated value chains as a widespread global model, and the increasing diversification, intensification and combination of financial mechanisms. Quite often, tools and models of value chain finance that were first developed by larger agribusinesses are now being adapted to include small farmers and small-to-medium scale agribusinesses. Therefore, the cases and learning collected here do not have a specific small-farmer emphasis although there is increasing application of value chain finance mechanisms for the benefit of smallholders, as illustrated in many of the examples.

The volume represents the extensive experience of many organizations, with the learning presented through case studies and descriptive analysis, followed by lessons learned and recommendations. The information is primarily drawn from a rich collection of documents, presentations and discussions that took place at international conferences on the subject that were organized by the FAO in Latin America, Africa, South Asia and Southeast Asia during 2006 and 2007, and research work in Eastern Europe and Central Asia in 2008. These conferences were organized in partnership with regional organizations on each continent. The information is augmented by learning from the research and case examples of multiple organizations who are working in this field.

The objective of the conferences was to learn more about practical experiences and approaches to value chain finance across countries. The conferences enabled a diverse set of participants to share and obtain information on best practices with the goal of increasing the supply and efficiency of financial services for rural producers, marketers and processors. Businesses active in the agricultural sector (including producers, processors, marketers and exporters) met together with leaders from financial institutions, technical assistance providers and policymakers to discuss this subject. Each region and country brought forth specific issues related to agricultural value chain finance, and these are noted in this volume. Overall, however, the concept and application of agricultural value chain finance has been shown to be consistent across regions.

An important part of each of the conference discussions was to analyse relevant policy issues: policy constraints, ways to improve policies, how to best perform in environments which lack desired policies for financing in the sector, and so on. These policy issues were reviewed from the distinctive perspectives of the many and varied types of stakeholders within a value chain, including those who provide the financing, investment and regulation.

We hope that this volume will serve as a practical primer on value chain finance for business and financial leaders, policymakers and practitioners, extension agents, universities and training institutes. We have strived to offer a rich learning opportunity by collecting, consolidating and presenting an array of relevant experiences from around the world.

CHAPTER 1
Introduction

'Agriculture continues to be a fundamental instrument for sustainable development and poverty reduction' (World Bank, 2008: 1–2); yet, 'financial constraints in agriculture remain pervasive, and they are costly and inequitably distributed, severely limiting smallholders' ability to compete' (ibid.: 13). Sudden and dramatic changes in food prices have exposed the vulnerability of agricultural production in meeting global demand and call for increased investment in agriculture at all levels. The question is how the right amount of investment can be acquired, particularly in a challenging milieu where financial uncertainty causes a reduction in available resources along with increased fear and scrutiny of risk. An answer to addressing these constraints goes beyond conventional measures since agriculture has always been difficult to finance through formal financial institutions and approaches.

The environment for agricultural finance is further influenced by the growing concentration of control in the agricultural sector. Driven by gains from economies of scale and globalization of the food chain along with access to resources, multinational and other interconnected agribusinesses have a greater impact in a sector that is characterized by increasing vertical and horizontal integration. The consequences of tightening integration are profound, especially for smallholders and others who are outside of the interlinked chains. In short, agriculture is evolving towards a modern, extremely competitive system driven by consumer demand for higher value, more processed products, and consistent quality and safety standards. Hence, enhancing smallholders' productivity, competitiveness and their participation in these global value chains have been noted as priorities of the agriculture-for-development agenda (World Bank, 2008).

Agricultural value chain finance offers an opportunity to reduce cost and risk in financing, and reach out to smallholder farmers. For financial institutions, value chain finance creates the impetus to look beyond the direct recipient of finance to better understand the competitiveness and risks in the sector as a whole and to craft products that best fit the needs of the businesses in the chain. Naturally, this more comprehensive approach to agricultural financing is not unique to value chain finance; some leading financial organizations in the sector employ such a focus in their loan assessment processes but this is more often not the case. In fact, much of the finance available to value chains is not from financial institutions but rather from others within the chain. At the same time, value chain finance can help the chains become more inclusive, by making resources available for smallholders to integrate into higher value markets. Finance that is linked with value chains is not new and some types of trader finance, for example, have been around for millennia; what is new is the way it is being applied more systematically to agriculture, using innovative or adapted approaches, tools and technologies. Examples of their application and innovation from around the world are shared and discussed in the following chapters.

Defining value chain finance

In our fast-paced development context, value chain finance is an evolving term that has taken on a range of meanings and connotations. The flows of funds to and among the various links within a value chain comprise what is known as *value chain finance*. Stated another way, it is any or all of the financial services, products and support services flowing *to and/or through* a value chain to address the needs and constraints of those involved in that chain, be it a need to access finance, secure sales, procure products, reduce risk and/ or improve efficiency within the chain. The comprehensive nature of value chain finance, therefore, makes it essential to analyse and fully understand the value chain in all aspects. The authors use the term here in reference to both internal and external forms of finance that are developing along with the agricultural value chains that they serve:

1. Internal value chain finance is that which takes place within the value chain such as when an input supplier provides credit to a farmer, or when a lead firm advances funds to a market intermediary.
2. External value chain finance is that which is made possible by value chain relationships and mechanisms: for example, a bank issues a loan to farmers based on a contract with a trusted buyer or a warehouse receipt from a recognized storage facility.

This discussion of value chain finance does not include conventional agricultural financing from financial institutions, such as banks and credit unions, unless there is a direct correlation to the value chain as noted above. Inevitably, there will be some grey areas in any such definition, and we recognize that financing approaches are often continuums through which an arbitrary line must be drawn for practical reasons of analysis and discussion.

An example of internal value chain finance is the case of input supplier credit in Myanmar where agro-input retailers offer deferred payment sales to smallholder farmers (Myint, 2007). A typical case of external value chain finance is exemplified in Kenya where small fruit and vegetable growers are able to access bank finance for agro-chemicals thanks to their export contract. The exporter pays the farmers through the bank, which deducts the scheduled loan payments before releasing the net proceeds to the farmer group (Marangu, 2007).

Value chain finance in agriculture must be seen in the light of the larger context, not only of the value chains proper but also the business environment of each country as this impacts value chains and the financial systems.

For this reason, the following two chapters provide background on the approach and the business models which have been developed around value chain finance. These chapters are followed by descriptions of financial instruments and innovations in value chain finance.

What is the interest around value chain finance in agriculture?

Value chain finance offers an opportunity to expand the financing opportunities for agriculture, improve efficiency and repayments in financing, and consolidate value chain linkages among participants in the chain. The specific opportunities that financing can create within a chain are driven by the context and business model and the relative roles of each participant in the chain. As stated by Campion (2006), finance often looks different when provided within a value chain than from a financial institution. Not only is the nature of the finance often different, but so are the motives. Nyoro (2007) notes that in Africa 'value chain actors are driven more by desire to expand markets than by the profitability of the finance'. Traders, for example, commonly use finance as a procurement facility while input suppliers often employ it as part of a sales incentive strategy. For financial institutions, it offers an approach to lower risk and cost in providing financial services. For the recipients of value chain finance, such as smallholder farmers or those purchasing their products, value chain finance offers a mechanism to obtain financing that may otherwise not be available due to a lack of collateral or transaction costs of securing a loan, and it can be a way to guarantee a market for products.

Understanding value chain finance can improve the overall effectiveness of those providing and requiring agricultural financing. It can improve the quality and efficiency of financing agricultural chains by: 1) identifying financing needs for strengthening the chain; 2) tailoring financial products to fit the needs of the participants in the chain; 3) reducing financial transaction costs through direct discount repayments and delivery of financial services; and 4) using value chain linkages and knowledge of the chain to mitigate risks of the chain and its partners. As agriculture and agribusiness modernize with increased integration and interdependent relationships, the opportunity and the need for value chain finance becomes increasingly relevant.

Overview of content

This book is built around actual case studies that were presented at a series of FAO conferences, which took place in Asia, Africa and Latin America in 2006 and 2007, as well as additional work in Eastern Europe and Central Asia in 2008. As a result of using real world examples, descriptions of specific financial models and instruments are often teased out of a complex system that exhibits a range of financial, agricultural, institutional, regulatory and sociocultural variables. As much as possible, illustrative cases have been streamlined to focus on a particular aspect of the system, and elaborate the topic under discussion. In some instances, a project or case may be used in more than one section to exemplify a relevant point.

The second chapter of this volume attempts to convey the current understanding of value chain finance as presented by practitioners and theorists in the field. The chapter begins with a section describing the contemporary agricultural context that is rapidly changing from fragmented and informal relationships to integrated and structured agribusiness systems. Based on an understanding of this context, agricultural value chain finance receives deeper analysis and definition in the next section. This leads to a discussion of value chain finance as an approach, not just a series of financial instruments, and ends with an examination of enabling environment issues including regulation and business and socio-economic contexts.

The third chapter elaborates four broad value chain business models – producer-driven, buyer-driven, facilitator-driven, and integrated – that provide a framework for understanding and analysing the structures and processes of agricultural value chains, and therefore the various applications of financing mechanisms that apply in different situations. Within these models specific mechanisms, such as contract farming which is growing rapidly in the developing world, are explained as they provide supportive structures through which value chain financing is often applied.

The next chapter, the fourth, provides a classification, definitions and examples of value chain finance mechanisms and tools from traditional products such as trader credit, to more complex instruments such as factoring. This core chapter of the volume explains the range of value chain finance tools and mechanisms, and illustrates them with a cross-section of mini-cases from highly differentiated agricultural systems around the globe.

Chapter five highlights and illustrates successful innovations in the application of models and financial tools. These include technological innovations as well as organizational and policy sector ones.

The final chapter looks at both general lessons and those for key applications and settings. Then it presents a set of recommendations, organized according to those for financial institutions, agribusiness firms and policymakers.

CHAPTER 2
Understanding agricultural value chain finance

Context

After many years of declining investment, there is renewed interest in agricultural financing. The rapid rise in food prices and a shortage of basic commodities experienced in 2008 has motivated increased attention from the public sector; the higher prices and consequently increased opportunity for profits is generating interest from the private sector. Investment decisions require placing much more emphasis on assessing the future trends and market potential. In addition, in an era of global markets, local supply and demand has less effect on prices as products more readily flow across borders, thus changing the nature of price risk within those markets.

The agro-food sector has undergone changes that have influenced new models of production and marketing involving a focus on demand rather than on producer-defined agricultural goods; a global, liberalized and fragmented marketplace with little seasonality and high product diversity; food safety and traceability requirements; and higher quality standards in conjunction with the enforcement of basic environmental regulations. This evolution requires a better understanding of the whole set of transactions within each value chain and that of the agricultural sector within which it operates. Integrated chains are able to do this most effectively. This information is important for making financial decisions.

Despite the changes in agriculture and agribusiness, the typical offer for financial products and services for agricultural and rural production has been deficient and not particularly innovative; financial intermediaries still lack much depth in rural areas, and producers, especially smallholders, are still underserved. Conventional thinking is that the agricultural sector is too costly and risky for lending. Yet, major banks in the sector such as Rabobank and Banorte, large financial institutions in the Netherlands and Mexico respectively, both express the view that agricultural credit is profitable if producers are well integrated into a viable value chain (Shwedel, 2007; Martínez, 2006).

It is recognized that increases in finance and investment are needed at all levels of the food chain, with special interest in increasing the access to finance by those agricultural households and communities who are most vulnerable to food insecurity and poverty. As such, although this book deals with agribusinesses of all sizes and types, significant consideration is given to the effects on small farmers and small agribusinesses that have the most to gain or lose in today's rapidly changing agricultural and economic environment.

Increasing finance and investment in a sustainable manner is not easy. Financing agriculture continues to be perceived as having high costs of operation, high risks and low returns on investment. Despite good intentions for directing credit to agriculture, the results of the agricultural lending programmes in developing countries commonly have unsatisfactory results with low rates of repayment in spite of (or often partly because of) high subsidies. Agricultural development banks have been slow to innovate, often due in part to governmental directives given to them. Commercial banks have traditionally shied away from this sector because of uncontrollable and systemic risks, higher costs and fear of the unknown for bankers not familiar with the sector and setting. The cost of directly lending to farmers, especially smaller ones, in hard-to-reach rural areas with less-educated and low-income populations is in fact generally prohibitive to most formal financial institutions. Microfinance institutions do reach some of these low-income households but at a high cost, with short-term loan products that are generally not able to address the full range of agricultural needs.

Even more important than the operational costs for transacting a loan or securing investments is the systemic or correlated risk in agriculture. This risk stems from both price volatility as well as from changeable weather patterns that can affect whole regions at a time, making repayment uncertain. In conventional lending, collateral is used to mitigate risks to the lender but the typical mortgage type of collateral commonly required by the banks is often not available or feasible in rural areas. This is due largely to land tenure restrictions and/or other requirements that are often designed to protect the livelihood assets of the community, but in doing so effectively limit their use as collateral. Hence, collateral is a major constraint to access to finance in agriculture not only from banks, but also from credit unions and other financing institutions. Central Bank policies can often exacerbate this constraint by requiring high reserves or imposing other restrictions which in effect penalize uncollateralized lending. Furthermore, the collapse of the global financial markets in 2008 and ensuing caution for financing activities with unknown and/or uncontrollable risk has led to financiers and investors requiring more assurance of markets, prices and controls.

Agriculture has been changing rapidly from one of fragmented production and marketing relationships toward integrated market systems, or chains. Driven by gains from economies of scale and globalization of the food chain, multinational agri-enterprises increasingly dominate the sector with more and more vertical and horizontal linkages or integration. The changes are also being driven by the marketplace and responsiveness to consumer interests, including stricter compliance, timeliness and quality standards. Agriculture, as with many other sectors, is now a *global* marketplace driven by competitiveness, which demands certain levels of efficiency and productivity. The future of farmers, traders and agribusinesses in the food or agro-industrial chain – and therefore the quality of their loan or investment – depends upon both their ability to compete in the marketplace and/or to adapt to markets in which they can compete. Further, success depends upon the collective competitiveness of everyone involved in the particular chain. In Kenya, Mrema (2007) notes that adoption of a value chain approach to agriculture begins with an attitude change by thinking in terms of 'we' instead of 'me' and focusing on harmonization of use of resources and interventions. Hence, the linkages, structure and overall health of the whole chain become much more important than ever before. Non-integrated, independent farmers, traders and businesses in a food system will likely become broken links in fragmented chains, unable to survive competition in the future.

Meeting the challenges of consumer trends and the demand for more processed or value added products requires increased investment in equipment, working capital, and skills and knowledge. Such investment is not only costly for individual value chain businesses, but can only be undertaken if there is an assurance from elsewhere in the chain for supplies, produce or markets. This creates the need to strengthen the links and commitment amongst value chain players, often through contracts. Agricultural transformation in the globalizing marketplace therefore not only creates new challenges but also new opportunities for using that integration to increase competitiveness and access to finance. Since more finance for agriculture is critical in meeting this challenge, it is hoped that financial institutions and policymakers can learn from and engage more with value chain actors in order to develop new products and to reach new markets.

Gonzalez-Vega (2007) raises a series of questions that a transformation and consolidation of agriculture would pose for finance:

1. Are financial systems in the countries prepared to meet the new demands for financial services arising from the growth of modern agro-food value chains? Will financial intermediaries be equipped to meet these demands and support the rapid growth of production and productivity triggered by the opportunities of globalization? To what extent will the success of the chains depend on progress toward widening the choice and access of rural financial services in these countries?

2. How much will the transformation of agriculture and the development of modern value chains shape the processes of financial access and delivery and the ability of financial intermediaries to meet resulting demands? Does the development of agricultural chains contribute new means of support for modernizing the financial system and how much does the emergence of contractual relationships among stakeholders benefit a country's financial development and outreach?

3. Will the supply of financial services that develops in response to these processes benefit all kinds of farmers? Which will be included, and which may not? How much will conventional financial systems be able to ease the incorporation of small- and medium-scale farmers into modern agricultural chains? Will the lack of access to financial services become an insurmountable barrier to entry for many traditional farmers?

What financial service options will be available to producers who are
not served by formal financial service providers?

This second set of questions in particular highlights the interplay between
agricultural development and the outreach of a country's financial systems.
In rural areas, there is a correlation between the number and development of
agribusinesses and financial institutions and vice versa. As agricultural value
chains become more sophisticated with responsive production to guaranteed
markets, financial institutions are able to act with reduced risk to increase
their services and further support the expansion and upgrading of agricultural
activities.

The effects of the growing integration of value chains also have important social implications as well as financial ones. It is therefore important to
analyse the effect of the vertical integration and market driven demand on
low-income producers, traders and processors. Enhancing their level of competitiveness and their participation in dynamic and profitable value chains are
two priorities of the agriculture-for-development agenda. With the fact that
the majority of the world's poor are in the agricultural and rural sectors, this
is an important development factor. Finance is important to value chains but
by itself is of little value. Even the most well-intentioned financial services
directed to agriculture will not be successful in the long run unless the producers and agribusinesses are competitive, not only today, but as the markets
evolve.

The concept of agricultural value chain finance

The value chain concept allows integration of the various players in agriculture production, processing and marketing. It defines the various roles
of players while at the same time, scope and purpose of partnerships that
can be established.
Equity Bank, Kenya (Muiruri, 2007)

The introduction of this book offered a definition of agricultural *value chain
finance* that takes into consideration the two broad aspects of its financing. It
is defined as both internal finance that takes place within the value chain and
external finance that is made possible by value chain relationships and mechanisms. This definition is enlarged in the following section, providing a detailed
examination of the term and its applications. It is also useful to note here that
the terms value chain and supply chain are often used interchangeably with
supply chain being used most frequently in industrial chains. For agriculture,
the term value chain is most appropriate for highlighting the value addition,
i.e. transformation of the inputs and products as they pass through the chain.
However first, we begin with an explanation of value chains proper.

The concept of 'agricultural value chain' includes the full range of activities
and participants involved in moving agricultural products from input suppliers to farmers' fields, and ultimately, to consumers' tables. Each stakeholder or

process in the chain has a link to the next in order for the processes to form a viable chain. At each stage, some additional transformation or enhancement is made to the product – ranging from simply moving the product from point 'a' to point 'b' (a common value addition of traders for example) to complex processing and packaging. Hence, a value chain is often defined as the sequence of value-adding activities, from production to consumption, through processing and commercialization. Each segment of a chain has one or more backward and forward linkages. A chain is only as strong as its weakest link and hence the stronger the links, the more secure the flow of products and services within the chain.

The 'farm to table' integration of a chain can increase efficiency and value through reduction of wastage, ensuring food safety, preserving freshness, decreasing consumer prices, and improving farmer prices and incomes. Efficient value chains normally reduce the use of intermediaries in the chain, and strengthen value-added activities because of better technology and inputs, farm gate procurement, upgraded infrastructure (such as cold chains), improved price opportunities through demand-driven production, and facilitation of more secure procurement for food processing and exports.

The flows of funds and internal and external financial arrangements among the various links in the chain comprise what is known as *value chain finance*. Stated another way, it is any or all of the financial services, products and support services flowing *to and/or through* a value chain. This can be internal financing directly from one value chain actor to another or external from a financial institution or investor based upon the borrower's value chain relations and activities.

The role of value chain finance is to address the needs and constraints of those involved in that chain. This is often a need for finance but it is also commonly used as a way to secure sales, procure products, reduce risk and/or improve efficiency within the chain. The comprehensive nature of value chain finance, therefore, makes it important to understand the nature of each chain, its actors and their interests. Some successful financial institutions have done this in their lending operations but many have not. Even fewer have multiparty financing arrangements in agriculture which is common in value chain finance among producers, suppliers, wholesalers and others.

A conceptual framework is useful for understanding value chain finance. This is important because value chain finance is both an *approach to financing* as well as a *set of financial instruments* which are utilized to expand and improve financial services to meet the needs of those involved in the value chain. Many of the instruments are not new but are often applied more broadly and frequently in combination with others. Most importantly, value chain finance is as an approach to financing that recognizes the entirety of the chain and the forces which drive it and responds accordingly to the specific requirements for financing them – the producers, traders, processors and others in the chain. It is a tailor-made approach which is designed to most efficiently meet the needs of the businesses and particular nature of the chain. These mechanisms and tools can be applied to: 1) finance production or harvest; 2) purchase inputs or products, or finance labour; 3) provide overdrafts or lines of credit; 4) fund investments; and 5) reduce risk and uncertainty. Therefore, value chain finance as an approach takes a systemic viewpoint, looking at the collective set of actors, processes and markets of the chain as opposed to an individual lender-borrower within the system. This is described in more detail in the next section.

Figure 2.1 presents a simplified framework for understanding value chain finance. As described above, it illustrates that finance is provided by those *within* the value chain itself, as well as by various types of institutional financing entities who provide financing *to* the chain. Products flow in one direction through the chain with varying levels of value addition at each level. Within the chain the finance flows in two directions, depending upon the particular value chain and/or region and the dynamics of the companies and participants involved. For example, in the rice industry, large wholesalers often finance traders who advance financing to the producers. At the same time, many processors receive unprocessed rice from farmers and producer groups

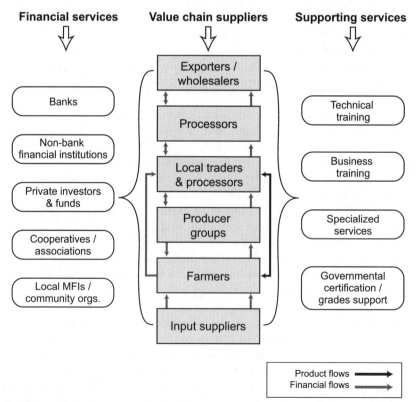

Figure 2.1 Product and financial flows within the value chain
Source: Adapted from Fries (2007) and Miller (2007a)

with only a partial payment with the understanding that final payment will be made after the rice is processed and sold. In this case the farmers are financiers to their rice millers.

It is noted in the figure that those within the chain can be both recipient users of finance as well as suppliers of finance. For example, an input supplier often receives financing to purchase inventory and sells the inputs on credit. Farmers may receive inputs on credit, they may receive advances from processors (directly or through their associations) and they may also provide in-kind finance, such as through delayed payments for their produce from millers, supermarkets or even governmental warehouses.

Box 2.1 highlights brief definitions of three interrelated value chain concepts. While the concept and approach of value chain finance may be quite new, the key components are not. The concept and practice of value chains or supply chains have been present for millennia, but in today's world of heightened market requirements and just-in-time delivery, the chains become ever more important. Similarly value chain analysis is a successor to the term subsector analysis and remains an important way of diagnosing a chain for determination of areas of weakness and intervention. It can also be noted that value chain finance and its increasing importance builds from the combination of value chain analysis, tailor designed financing, increased market integration in agriculture and the application of improved financial instruments and information technologies. It commonly involves multiple parties, each of which have a vested interest in the success of the others in the chain – the more each have to gain or lose from the partnership, the stronger the value chain. These relationships can be formal or informal. They can involve simple financing agreements such as with the traditional 'farming on shares' where

---

Box 2.1 Value chain definitions

A useful starting point for understanding value chain financing in agriculture is with three general definitions:

1. Value chain – the set of actors (private, public, and including service providers) and the sequence of value-adding activities involved in bringing a product from production to the final consumer. In agriculture they can be thought of as a 'farm to fork' set of processes and flows (Miller and da Silva, 2007).
2. Value chain analysis – assessment of the actors and factors influencing the performance of an industry, and relationships among participants to identify the driving constraints to increased efficiency, productivity and competitiveness of an industry and how these constraints can be overcome (Fries, 2007).
3. Value chain finance – financial services and products flowing to and/or through value chain participants to address and alleviate driving constraints to growth (Fries, 2007).

To summarize, the key aspects of the value chain definitions for agriculture are:

o   Value chains – multiple, linked actors and sequential, value-adding activities.
o   Value chain analysis – assessment of actors, relationships, constraints and opportunities.
o   Value chain finance – finance to address the constraints and opportunities, both through the value chain, and to and/or because of the value chain.

costs, inputs and returns are shared. In this case, through informal or contractual arrangements, a farmer typically receives inputs such as seeds, fertilizer and technical guidance, in exchange for a share in the product with a business partner – who may be a neighbour or an agribusiness wanting to secure produce for their mill or business.

A study by the Temeo Institute demonstrated that in Kenya, as in many parts of Africa, the use of value chain finance has been a common part of the production and marketing systems of major commodities, both in the tea plantations that were set up centuries ago and in more recent structures. For example, the last century saw governmental schemes involving marketing boards, inputs and directed credit lines. The latter started in the 1930s with the creation of the National Advances Board which made available public funds for lending to farmers and for supervision of lending. These advances were made against land and the crop that was financed as collateral. The Kenya case in Figure 2.2 shows the inter-relation of the governmental Agricultural Finance Corporation (AFC) providing inputs through the Kenya Farmers Association (KFA) and cash to farmers who in turn sold their production output to the governmental National Cereals Produce Board (NCPB).

The NCPB discounted loan payments owed to the AFC and the remaining funds were repaid back to the farmers. During this time in Kenya, the AFC was in effect the only government organization that provided finance in agriculture. The AFC was financed by the government and grants and loans from international donors. Although costly, the government offered both credit and complimentary supportive services to farmers as shown in Table 2.1. The combined effect produced both stability and stimulus to growth in the agricultural sector. However, in the post reform period of agricultural finance, the integrated system began to decompose with some of the changes and effects noted below.

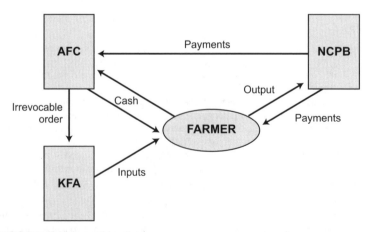

Figure 2.2 Interlinked cereal lending
Source: Nyoro (2007)

Table 2.1 Kenyan Government Interlinked Cereal programme

Interlinked Cereal programme lending and services	Effects

• Governmental financing in agriculture for:
  o capital purchases, including land;
  o farm machinery;
  o seasonal credit.
• Subsidized inputs;
• Market access and price controls;
• Extension services;
• Infrastructural development.
	• High economic and agricultural growth rates of 6 per cent per annum;
	• Comparatively the highest adoption rates for hybrid seeds and fertilizers;
	• Local income growth;
	• High cost to national budget to maintain AFC.

Kenyan post reform agricultural finance	
Changes	**Effects**
• Elimination of price controls for commodities; • Discontinuation of integrated credit programmes; • Break-down of interlinked credit; • Political interference on lending and recovery.	• Producers exposed to price risks; • High default rates on lending by AFC; • Side-selling of agricultural commodities; • Withdrawal of commercial banks from rural areas.

Notwithstanding the many valid reasons for the discontinuation of the former governmental approach to integrated chains in agriculture used in Kenya, there are two important features to note. First, the 'full-service' approach and the stability of prices promoted growth in income and use of technology, albeit at high cost. It also provided security for lending and for marketing procurement. When these were no longer available with the discontinuation of the interlinked programme, the result was an increase in lending default and breach of sales contracts (side-selling).

A similar situation resulted with the breakdown of the Soviet Union. When the state-controlled integrated value chains, often extending between countries, were severed, markets became unreliable and financing became unavailable. Only when value chain integration began to be developed by the private sector, did financing begin to flow again, often using value chain finance approaches and instruments as a way to access financial resources.

It is also important to note that value chain finance is not a replacement for mainstream financial service providers such as banks and credit unions. These remain very important for providing finance and other financial services to the chain actors. The approach and tools used in value chain finance build on and enhance informal credit and conventional, collateral-based financing through banks and other financial institutions to offer a full complement of financing products. For example, traders commonly provide finance to farmers for harvest, inputs or other needs both related to the agricultural chain or household during the production cycles such as advances to cover emergencies. Many of these traders in turn receive finance from millers and processors who in turn may be financed by banks and/or wholesalers or exporters who are farther along the supply or value chain. Although they often use conventional financing institutions, rural producers, processors and retailers are receiving increasingly large injections of resources from other entities with which they maintain trade ties.

The amount of funding that flows upward in the value chain should not be underestimated since it is significant. Agro-input suppliers providing seeds and inputs on credit, farmers who deliver products to warehouses or processors with delayed payments and wholesalers who sell to supermarkets on consignment or with delayed payments are among the most common examples.

Agricultural value chain finance as an approach

Value chain finance can be viewed as a series of tools and mechanisms, yet, most importantly it is an approach that takes a systemic viewpoint, looking at the collective set of actors, processes and markets of the chain as opposed to an individual lender-borrower within the system. Decisions about financing are based on the health of the entire system, including market demand, and not just on the individual borrower. This means that in order to offer value chain-based finance, knowledge of the agricultural system is required.

In other forms of finance, whether internal financing within the chain, such as traditional trader credit, or financing originating externally, such as conventional banking finance, the view is less comprehensive, and therefore incorporates significant risk. The additional risk is due in large part to 'uncertainty'; not being able to fully understand the risks and consequently not being able to assess and mitigate against those risks. Uncertainty also leads to a higher perception of risk causing conventional lending to the sector to be reduced.

Shwedel states, 'Chain-based financing requires the banker to see and understand the business in its entirety. It demands adjustment to new market conditions, more accurate pricing, a better understanding of risk, and consequently, a greater willingness to take risk' (2007: 22). In his work as value chain finance specialist for Rabobank Mexico, he has learned that with a holistic understanding of the chain, there is potential to reduce risk and open up the doors to finance based on systemic knowledge.

Box 2.2 Flower chain financing, Mexico

In the case of flower producers in Mexico, Rabobank finances their needs for working capital, equipment and technology. Closely aligned with this, Rabobank also finances the equipment distributor who provides needed technology to the farmers. The bank finances the farmers because the bank knows them and understands their marketing system. In fact, the farmers send their products to an auction market in Holland, and Rabobank finances the auction market and many of the buyers in the market. In this way, the bank has locked up the financing of the whole chain and has intimate knowledge of the chain – production factors, equipment suppliers, and buyers. The bank also knows that the farmers receive their money as it is deposited in a Rabobank account, so that the bank can directly debit their accounts for loan payments.

Source: Shwedel (2007)

An example of the Rabobank approach is highlighted in Box 2.2 that describes the financing of flowers which are considered a specialized, high-risk sector in Mexico.

As in the Rabobank case, a lender is more likely to give a loan to a farmer when that farmer is connected to a viable buyer, and when the buyer in turn has solid market access. Most businesses and financial institutions do not have the global reach of Rabobank, but through strong linkages among partners and follow-up of flows of product and funds, they can achieve the necessary understanding and control needed to minimize risks and have competitive efficiency in their value chain financing. In the past, without such value chain knowledge and interconnectivity, the farmers or small processors and traders may have been more readily refused a loan and therefore unable to finance their operations to take advantage of a market opportunity. The familiarity of the players in a specific chain with each other supports the promotion and development of effective arrangements that facilitate financing. The main purpose is sharing risks among various actors, transferring defined risks to those parties that are best equipped to manage them, and as far as possible, reducing costs through direct linkages and payments.

Since value chain finance is built not only upon physical linkages but also through knowledge integration, a key to success for financial institution is to 'know the business'. Those who know the business the best are those persons and companies directly involved in the value chain. Having and using specialized knowledge of the chain, financiers and investors can understand the risks and work to mitigate them more easily than a conventional banker who works with all types of businesses and clients. This ability and commitment to analysing and using the value chain, enables financial institutions to tailor appropriate financial products and services to the participants in the value chain. Success in this field depends upon making use of this collective body of knowledge followed by subsequent tailoring or structuring of traditional and non-traditional financial mechanisms and tools to fit the value chain. The main purpose is sharing risks among various actors and transferring defined risks to those parties that are best equipped to manage them. Hence, the value chain finance approach is a process of building and using knowledge to determine financial services and interventions. The actual financing can be either direct from one chain partner to another, indirect by a third party financial institution or 'cascading', meaning financing enters the chain to partners at multiple levels according to the activities in the chain.

Whereas, conventional financing relies heavily on the creditworthiness of the client and business, value chain financing focuses more on the payments to be received from activities, such as production and value-added transactions. This allows for increased access to finance for those without sufficient collateral but with predictable flows of goods, and strong partners in the chain. Moreover, in many cases, the transactions can be structured such that the repayment of a loan is automatically made via the transaction proceeds. This direct form of loan repayment, reduces both repayment risk as well as transaction costs of loan repayment. Each participant in a value chain has a different capacity to obtain financing and the conditions vary accordingly. Their common interest is in obtaining finance easily under favourable conditions; whether it comes from a bank, supplier or trader is not important. If, for example, a major buyer can obtain financing and advance funds to others in the chain at less overall cost, everyone benefits.

Following a value chain finance approach, the loan analysis for a specific borrower comprehensively considers the many aspects and processes of the value chain, including who within the chain is best placed to be the borrower(s), and what are the flows of funds and from whom. Kariuki states that the key issues for consideration in value chain finance in the Cooperative Bank of Agriculture are: 1) the strength of the value chain and its opportunities and challenges; 2) the risks; 3) the technical, business and financial services and support, and 4) the business model for value chain finance (Mwangi, 2007). In essence, the process involves a combination of value chain assessment, financial assessment and securing agreements. A few key steps that can be employed by such an institution are:

1. Understand the value chain:
   o Enabling environment – international, regional and domestic enabling environment, regulatory constraints and opportunities for support;
   o Vertical and horizontal relationships – linkages between levels of the chain and competitors and with those on the same level, their interests and commitment;
   o Support markets and services – financial and non-financial services, and input supply markets;
   o End market – market potential, consumer demands and chain risks (adaption from Coop, 2008).
2. Identify the value chain model that currently exists – lead actors, business model and sustainability strategy;
3. Identify the transaction processes – value added in the various stages of the product up the value chain;
4. Determine actual and critical points of finance – the current flows of funds and their sources of financing, what is needed and in what point in time;
5. Analyse and compare financing options – their relative strengths, risks and costs of financing for each level of participant in the chain;
6. Design financing according to the best option(s) to fit the chain – draw up agreements for financing between parties.

While much of the emphasis in a value chain finance approach is on the health of the chain and its value-adding transactions and linkages, a well-rounded assessment of all borrowers is still critical. This borrower assessment can be undertaken by looking at key areas commonly called the 5 C's of loan assessment. These refer to: 1) character; 2) capacity; 3) capital; 4) collateral;

Box 2.3 Five C's of lending applied to value chain financing

1. Character   • Suppliers, producers, purchasers and others in a value chain who inter-
act regularly can assess the character and management savvy of each
other better than a banker, with whom they have infrequent interaction.

2. Capacity   • Assessment is broadened from the borrower's individual capacity toward
a focus on the health and growth potential of the value chain and the
competitiveness of those involved in it; also an individual's borrowing
capacity can be strengthened because they are integrated into a strong
value chain.

3. Capital   • The capital of the borrower alone is less emphasized in value chain
finance, as increased attention is given to the capitalization within the
whole chain.

4. Collateral   • Cash and commodity flows which can be predicted from past relations
or contracts can replace or enhance traditional collateral; also in tightly
integrated chains the collateral of the strongest partners can be used for
attracting finance, which can also be a benefit to others in the chain.

5. Conditions   • Conditions for financing are more adapted to the chain; tailoring finance
to fit the specific needs becomes paramount to its success and can
improve 'bankability' of the clients.

Source: Miller (2008a)

---

and 5) conditions (Miller, 2008a). Banks have typically given highest priority
to collateral and in microfinance the focus of priority is to character and capacity. These remain important in loan assessment but, as shown in Box 2.3,
their relative level of importance changes as does the breadth of the assessment to go beyond that of the immediate borrower.

In value chain finance, increased importance is given to the conditions of
both the market outlook and the fit of the financial requirements to the needs
and flows of the chain. The 'fit' of the financial conditions and cash flows to
those clients within the chain is critical and assessment of the risks of break-
downs in the chain form part of the analysis. The cash flow of the value chain
must be sufficient and in total synch with that of the loan conditions. The
capacity of the partners as well as the borrower is also importance. Hence, a
risk assessment moves well beyond client credit risk and requires assessment
of the risks of market, price and production.

Does this mean that the bank or financier must assess and fully understand
everything in the value chain? No, most do not have such capacity except in
the chains with which they are dealing closely, but rather they can often rely
in part on the strength and reputation of the strongest actors in the chain.
Most often these are larger businesses farther up the chain with strong credit
histories who are experts in the chains in which they operate.

Enabling environment

The collection of institutions, policies, attitudes and support services that define
the setting where enterprises operate is known as the enabling environment, or

business climate. The constituting elements of an enabling environment in any given economy are multi-faceted, covering themes such as the rule of law, public sector governance, overall macro-economic conditions, infrastructure and regulations affecting business, and socio-cultural context among others. Governments and international organizations are now paying increased attention to the assessment and promotion of reforms of enabling environments, having acknowledged that a conducive business climate is an essential pre-requisite for investments in new enterprises and for the sustained growth and competitiveness of the existing ones. The World Bank 'Doing Business' survey (World Bank, 2009) has been established as an authoritative benchmark in this area of concern, generating country rankings that have been instrumental in engendering business climate reforms worldwide.

The application of value chain finance depends upon the environment in which it operates. As with all finance, the starting point is to have the conditions for profitable business activity with some level of stability. Within finance, some financial instruments can only be applied if certain regulations or compliance is in place. Macro-economic instability or erratic policies adversely affect risk perceptions and undermine the potential of value chain financing instruments. Yet, at other times, value chain financing serves as a method of alternative finance when conditions for loans and services from conventional sources such as banks are not in place. For this reason the business models for value chains and their financing are developed according to the operating conditions and the characteristics of those involved in the chain.

More often than not, work on building an enabling environment requires interventions on multiple levels in order to be effective. For example, in Tanzania, IFAD found that reforms were needed on three levels described by Cherogony (2007) as follows:

- *Macro level* is the policy level that creates an enabling environment (warehouse receipt act, taxation and marketing policy);
- *Meso level* takes into consideration private sector intermediaries (insurance, collateral managers, commercial banks);
- *Micro level* involves various local and 'grassroots' institutional forms from farmer associations and community based microfinance institutions (SACCOS).

Some of the elements of enabling environments that are of particular relevance for the successful design and implementation of value chain financing initiatives are briefly discussed in the next section. Interested readers will find additional information on this topic in the series of documents prepared by the Rural Infrastructure and Agro-industries Division of FAO on enabling environments for agribusiness and agro-industries development (see FAO website, www.fao.org/ag/ags/subjects/en/agribusiness).

Standards and certification

Among the elements that constitute an enabling environment, quality and safety standards appear as an item of increasing relevance. Indeed, a major driver in the integration of agricultural value chains has come from the introduction of quality and safety standards and the demands for strict compliance by buyers of agro-food products. In modern agro-food systems, chain linkage has become a requirement in many sectors, due to consumer requirements for higher standards for food quality and safety and year-round availability. The unorganized chains cannot meet those demands.

Standards for food products are in two categories: 1) those relating to food safety, which may require certification to demonstrate concurrence of meeting the minimum standards; and 2) those relating to the intrinsic value of the product. The latter include quality, variety, size, shape, etc., as well as brand which is normally determined by the industry norms and companies themselves. Timeliness of delivery is another company-imposed standard to meet market demands. Niche market characteristics that include their own set of standards, such as for organic produce and regional specific branding (e.g. French Champagne), are also becoming more important and have demonstrated an opportunity for some operators.

Tracing, to track the origin of products and their pathway through the value chain, has been shown to be of increasing importance for both safety as well as branding. This can only be feasible through well-structured and linked value chains. For small producers, such changes in the marketplace requirements make it increasingly difficult to compete unless they are well organized and linked with or integrated into strong agricultural value chains. Many of these changes which started with export agriculture are now being introduced at the local level. The following illustrates the importance of standards and their formalization in Kenyan horticulture markets:

> Recognizing the importance of standards and certification for competitiveness in the fresh produce industry, The Fresh Produce Export Association of Kenya (FPEAK) coordinated efforts to develop 'Kenya GAP' standards. With its emphasis on quality standards, food safety and traceability, customized to Kenyan conditions for both large and small-scale growers, it also reduces risk to all in the value chain as well as financiers since all are vulnerable if unsafe or low-quality products affect the market. (Wairo, 2007)

Finance and investment from banks and other financial institutions to producers or agribusinesses face a major risk if there is not adequate attention given to the standards of quality and safety of the products. This involves not only their clients who borrow, but also the compliance to standards among all participants within the value chains of their clients. Everyone is affected positively or negatively by the actions of their chain partners.

Financing within the value chain from one partner to another can have the effect of providing incentives or penalties for achievement, or not, of the targets for specified standards. To encourage improved product quality or timeliness, for example, finance can be advanced for irrigation, improved packaging and storage or improved inputs. For those who do not meet standards, advance financing can be withheld and/or payment delayed, reduced or refused.

Regulation and enforcement

Regulation for supporting value chain finance is two-fold: having proper regulations and enforcing them. Governments play an important function in setting the guiding principles for agriculture and agribusiness, as well as for the rules that govern finance. In value chain finance the product-related standards noted above must not only be set for countries and globally, they must be enforced in order to ensure transparency, consistency and compliance. Not only is the reputation of the product and the country's product at stake, but there is also the need for consistency in order to provide the ability to trade effectively and co-mingle products. Standard sized bags or weights, standard grades and regulated processes for insuring safety, for instance, must be enforced in order for value chains to be efficient.

Regulation and enforcement are both a public and private issue. In many food sectors such as fruits and vegetables, private companies and their industry associations impose regulations which are much stricter than governmental ones, either to meet international or supermarket requirements or to maintain a quality standard. They may also be in a position to enforce the regulations better than the state judicial system because of a mutual interest among partners in the chain to maintain good working relations for the future.

In value chain financing arguably the most difficult area for regulation and enforcement is contract enforcement, which is critical for ensuring follow-through of commitments. It is noted, for example, if farmers are allowed to break contracts and side-sell to outsiders when the price is better, or if buyers are allowed to renege on purchases (or provide other control barriers) when their price contracted is disadvantageous, then the systems fail and all in the chain are affected. In Uganda, for example, it was shown that 'governance structures that encourage long-term interdependent relationships generally facilitate increased access to finance' (Johnston and Meyer, 2008). The same holds true for countries which can shut off imports and cause problems or even failure for those actors in value chains dependent upon their market.

Banking regulation is often geared toward conventional, collateral-based lending and regulation that can address the less common forms of loan security such as product-based financing security. This is often lacking, thus limiting the use of some of the value chain financial products. Yet the required regulation can be developed. When considering the example of microfinance for which new regulation was developed, a similar expansion of regulation can be expected to meet the requirements of value chain financing. Moreover, many of the key issues relating to regulation are not unique to agricultural value chain finance. This is illustrated here in the summary of the key value chain financing issues to be addressed, as identified by the African bankers and central bankers at the AFRACA Agribanks Forum in 2007. Of these priority issues, only the first two are unique to value chain finance:

Financial regulation:
- Expand the policy environment for agricultural and rural finance to cover the emerging financial products and technologies;
- Assess and improve policies aimed at enhancing warehousing services and warehouse receipt financing.

Business environment:
- Prioritize increased expenditures on research and rural infrastructure in the agricultural sector;
- Improve financial sector policies for economic and exchange rate stability;
- Improve the environment for private financial investment, including tax policies and concessions when appropriate to strengthen profitable farming systems.

Equality:
- Enhance smallholders' access to markets;
- Enforce transparency and fair treatment of all players;
- Build capacity for value chain clientele to meet standards and regulations.

Macro-economic and social context

As indicated previously, one of the main considerations for agricultural financing and value chain development is the overall environment. Some international organizations, such as the World Bank, consider the policy environment above all other factors (Tiffen, 2006). For example, in some economies a particular value chain that aims at international markets might be weakly developed, but can be rapidly expanded if the general macro-economic environment under which it operates improves, perhaps by reforms in exchange rate or trade policies. In others, well functioning chains might lose competitiveness if affected negatively by misguided interventions in areas such as taxes (fiscal policy) or interest rates (monetary policies) that distort competition among sectors or between countries.

Other variables in the general business context are important and wide-ranging for financing of agricultural value chains to be effective or even feasible. Questions such as the following can elicit important information in value chain development: Is the private sector vibrant? Are there regional disparities to be considered? Are there a range of services and infrastructure available to support agricultural value chain development from inputs to transportation and packaging? What is the outreach and availability of financial products for addressing value chain needs?

Financing to agriculture has always been susceptible to political interests. In many instances, loans have been made for political motives, collection has been difficult due to the inability or reluctance to prosecute those unwilling to repay, and loans have been forgiven or granted moratoriums on repayment, all of which lead to an unwillingness to lend to agriculture. Value chain finance is less affected by loans being forgiven or politically dictated interest rates, since these are commonly embedded into the marketing contracts and payment is often secured by product. However, it is not immune to political intervention and as noted in the previous section, the social and political context for dealing with contract breaking, such as side-selling, is arguably the most important issue that can limit the use of value chain financing.

Socio-economic factors of the country as a whole and the particular characteristics of each value chain also play an important role in the nature of financing within and to agricultural value chains. Issues such as gender, ethnicity, class, caste and religion can impact the role and status of players, their ability to access services including finance, and the way in which services can be offered. In some countries, for example, fruit and vegetables and dairy are value chains managed largely by women while major commodities and livestock are managed by men. Some products may also be more recently introduced and more readily organized as modern chains, while others are age-old commodities and can be more difficult. For example, in Bolivia, beans as a commercial crop were introduced less than 20 years ago and local marketing and export use standard weights and grades, have a well-organized National Bean Producers Organization (ASOPROF) and integrated value chains, much of which is exported to established buyers. Potato marketing, on the other hand, uses a centuries-old system of weights, no standard grading system and has a fragmented marketing structure of many small buyers, spot-market prices and insecurity of payment. In this regard it is much more difficult to apply value chain finance when the chain is not organized or standardized.

In Muslim countries, Islamic finance is often practised and specific financial products have been developed accordingly. Some of the Islamic finance products have equivalent features to some of the principles and products of value chain financing in that the borrowers in Islamic banking transactions are considered business partners who can jointly bear the risks and profits. For example, Islamic *Murabaha* lending is similar to trade financing with buy-resell contracts. *Ajaar* lending involves lease-purchase agreements and *Mu'ajjal* involves advance sales with deferred delivery contracts (Miller, 2007b).

The context of each value chain is distinct. For those with less stringent requirements (as is often the case for unprocessed, durable commodities such as beans and rice) the level of organization of the value chain and its business context have less effect than is the case for the export foodstuffs such as fruits and vegetables. These have strict needs and without adequate assurance of facilities for moving the product to market, these products will spoil. If there is not delivery compliance and secure payment systems, the opportunities for extending finance of any type will vanish.

Box 2.4 Financial flows within the rice industry

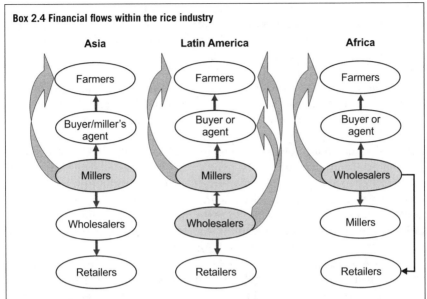

The most significant differences in value chain financing are not between regions and countries but rather across sectors and their value chains. However, each region and country does have specific differences. This is noted, for example, in who is the lead firm within a value chain, and how finance plays an important role in their taking a lead. For example, Gálvez demonstrated that FAO case studies in the rice chain found that millers played the central financing role for rice in Asia and wholesalers were central in financing within the rice chain in Africa.

Source: Gálvez (2006a)

Moreover, the structure of a value chain and the roles of its actors in the same sector may vary within regions. An example of this is shown in Box 2.4.

Value chains and diversified livelihoods

In a global economy, livelihoods are no longer simply dependent upon what one produces, but also how that production fits with competitive chains in the market system. The emphasis on global systems that has developed is useful in the context of understanding the intricacies of each chain even at the local level. Even so, from a livelihood perspective as well as a financial viewpoint, it is important to understand the status of a chain from the vantage of each participant within a chain. Diversification of activities among multiple chains is noted as important to both farmers, agro-processors and traders to reduce not only product and market risks but also to level seasonality requirements for labour, equipment and capital as described by Medlicott in Honduras who notes that 'diversification puts producers in a more sustainable position by reducing market and production risks. Yet at the same time it permits them to maximize resources and activities on a year-a-round basis, thus incrementing their income, reducing fixed costs and providing continuous employment.' (Medlicott presentation, in Quirós, 2007)

For agro-processors, an overdependence on a particular chain can also be detrimental if not hedged or diversified adequately. For financial institutions, it may seem counter-intuitive to say that an agricultural value chain finance approach looks beyond the chain, but this is not the case for several reasons. First, the value chain approach helps to understand the risks and diversify lending portfolios accordingly to reduce systemic risks change production, price and even political. Secondly, a careful understanding of a sub-sector helps to assess the potential for those involved to move across chains as the market changes and/or to adjust to these market changes. For example, the linkages between farmer organizations, warehouses and financing systems can be used for maize as well as beans and other products.

As shown in the diagram below, value chain development and its financing can be integrated into a comprehensive livelihood model. For small farmers in India, this was found to be important for insuring sustainable and profitable farming and hence loan repayment. Finance is one of several value chain services required to enhance competencies, increase outreach, reduce transaction costs and reduce risk for farmers and stakeholders. In the BASIX model, these include inputs supplies, output markets, research and technology, group

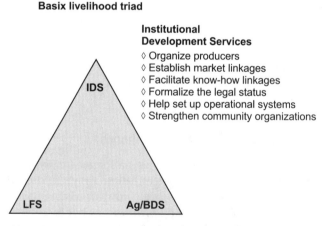

Basix livelihood triad

Institutional Development Services

◊ Organize producers
◊ Establish market linkages
◊ Facilitate know-how linkages
◊ Formalize the legal status
◊ Help set up operational systems
◊ Strengthen community organizations

IDS

LFS   Ag/BDS

Livelihood Financial Services

• Savings and credit
• Insurance for lives and livelihoods
• Fund transfers
• Commodity derivatives
• Financial development

Agricultural Business Development Services

» Productivity enhancement
» Risk mitigation (non-insurance)
» Local value addition
» Alternative input and sales linkages

Figure 2.3 BASIX livelihood services model

organization, training and extension services as well as financial services (Ramana, 2007a).

Agriculture is the livelihood of the majority of the world's poor and is an important development concern. Both private and public sector intervention needs to be addressed. These include:

- Pre-harvest: 1) quality agricultural inputs; 2) updated knowledge; 3) contract farming; 4) future price options; and 5) crop risk mitigation.
- Post-harvest: 1) warehouse receipts linked to loans; 2) local value addition; 3) linkages to markets; 4) aggregation; and 5) farm-to-end-user, i.e. value chain linkages. (Ramana, 2007a)

Models that are supportive of value chain financing are described in the following chapter. In all such models, the diversity of activities and services used in one value chain are often applied to multiple chains within a business or a farm in order to reduce overdependence on one chain.

CHAPTER 3
Value chain business models

For an enterprise, the term *business model* refers to the way it creates and captures value within a market network of producers, suppliers and consumers, or, in short, 'what a company does and how it makes money from doing it' (Vorley, 2008). The business model concept is linked to business *strategy* (the process of business model design) and business *operations*. For a value chain, the use of the phrase *business model* refers to the drivers, processes and resources for the entire system, even if the system is comprised of multiple enterprises. If finance is to be successful, the value chain must be viewed as a single structure, and the model of this structure provides a framework for further analysis.

Understanding how a value chain is structured and coordinated can reduce risk and hesitancy of financial intermediaries to lend to the agricultural sector. Figure 3.1 describes different value chain structures, defined in terms of the relationship between two stakeholders: buyer and seller. The buyers are agricultural processors, exporters or distributors, or in some cases, supermarkets. Sellers are the producers or traders who sell their products to these buyers along the chain.

The relationship between these two stakeholders, buyer and seller, can be described through five types of linkages: 1) the instant or spot market, where producers come to sell their commodities, and prices fluctuate; this is the most risky in terms of setting market price; 2) a contract to produce and buy, known more generally as contract farming; 3) a long term often informal relationship characterized by trust or interdependency; 4) a capital investment by one of the buyers for the benefit of the producer, characterized by high levels of

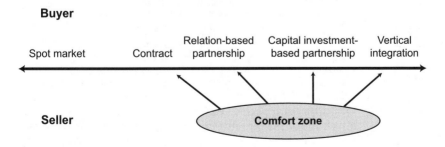

Figure 3.1 Different ways to coordinate and structure the value chain
Source: Wenner (2006)

producer credibility and dependence; and 5) a company that has achieved full vertical integration. When production and marketing is dependent upon a spot market with fluctuating prices and demands, financiers are uneasy; they prefer a contractual or partnership structure in a value chain where the market risks can be more controlled. This is their comfort zone.

As noted in the introduction, although agricultural value chain finance deals with a range of agribusinesses and other chain partners who are both large and small, value chain finance is particularly useful in helping link small farmers and agribusinesses into effective market systems. With models that promote economies of scale and reduce risks for lenders and buyers, small-holder farmers are more viable contributors to modern agricultural systems. Because smallholder production is important in many value chains for both economic and social considerations, special emphasis must be given to models which allow them to fully participate in value chains. The following table, adapted from Vorley (2008), illustrates the typical organization of smallholder production and marketing – that is, the relation of farmers to the market and/or the larger system. This analysis offers a basis for value chain business models, and the accompanying finance, which is expanded upon in the following sections.

The following sections elaborate on this categorization, providing descriptions and illustrations of each model. The models are characterized by the main driver of the value chain, and its rationale or objective. For example, it was noted earlier in Box 2.4 that millers are often the drivers of the rice chain in order to assure supply and increase volume, typical characteristics of a buyer-driven model.

Table 3.1 Typical organizational models of smallholder production

Model	Driver of organization	Rationale
Producer-driven (Association)	• small-scale producers, especially when formed into groups such as associations or cooperatives; • large scale farmers.	• access new markets; • obtain higher market price; • stabilize and secure market position.
Buyer-driven	• processors; • exporters; • retailers; • traders, wholesalers and other traditional market actors.	• assure supply; • increase supply volumes; • supply more discerning customers – meeting market niches and interests.
Facilitator-driven	• NGOs and other support agencies; • national and local governments.	• 'make markets work for the poor'; • regional and local development.
Integrated	• lead firms; • supermarkets; • multi-nationals.	• new and higher value markets; • low prices for good quality; • market monopolies.

Producer-driven value chain models

Producer associations are a critical component of many value chains. In certain cases, the association becomes the driver for value chain development – providing technical assistance, marketing, inputs and linkages to finance. In other cases, the association may have a financial base, such as Credinka in the following example, whereby a savings and loan association signs a contract with farmers to guarantee sale of their product. Credinka is part of a much more complex system of interrelated associations that support the cacao value chain in Peru, providing contractual arrangements, finance, processing, market access, inputs and training.

Producer-driven models are driven from the bottom end of the chain. They can be successful but face two major difficulties. First, producers may not understand the market needs as well as those in the chain who are closer to the end user. Secondly, producers often struggle for financing unless they can find strong partners and/or can get assistance for financing (such as the case of

---

Box 3.1 Cacao producer association, Peru

INDACO, or Industria Alimentaria 'La Convención', was founded in 1994 as a business initiative of Cáritas, an outreach organization of the Roman Catholic Church. The partners are a consortium of public and private institutions interested in furthering agroindustry development in the region. Aprocav is a 3,500 member cacao farmer association that is the majority shareholder of INDACO. Aprocav consolidates the crop, lends technical assistance and sells the harvest to INDACO, which processes it into cacao butter, cacao powder and glazes. INDACO's largest project, the cacao plant, embodies an investment of over US$1.5 million and was built with support from the Inter-American Development Bank.

Credinka is a Rural Savings and Loan Association (CRAC) founded in 1994 by the federation of coffee cooperatives in Peru. After two or three years, INDACO and Aprocav joined the savings and loan association, and today are the second largest group of shareholders. The savings and loan association is under the supervision of the Superintendence of Banks and is a member of Peru's formal financial system. It has equity worth approximately US$2 million, making it the fifth largest of the 12 CRACs in Peru. It has four offices, more than US$11 million in deposits and nearly US$14 million in loans. Credinka provides agricultural supply loans of up to US$3,000 for farmers who are members of producer associations. Specifically, in order to receive their credit, farmers must be members of Aprocav or Ecomusa (another farmer association that functions as a community enterprise), and have the backing of either of these institutions. Loans are guaranteed by the farmers' sponsoring institutions and are regulated by means of a report that is prepared and submitted by the technical personnel of the different associations, stipulating the amount to be lent to each farmer.

In order to obtain their loan guarantee, farmers must sign a contract with the association, pledging to sell the entire cacao crop in exchange for an above-market price that pays a premium for production quality. Aprocav and Ecomusa sell the crops to INDACO to be processed and marketed. Finally, the associations repay Credinka for the loans to farmers, and the balance is deposited directly in the farmers' account with the rural savings and loan. For processing and marketing, INDACO has set up a fund with resources from Credinka, the United Nations, the Inter-American Development Bank, private banks and its own equity.

Source: Melosevic in Quirós (2007: 74–76)

Credinka) and fore-linking to reliable and competitive markets and partners. While the start-up years are particularly difficult for these and other reasons – e.g., lack of capacity and economies of scale – with time and support, producer models can become strong and begin to access financing based upon the strength of their transaction flows and market partners. The many strong coffee cooperatives in Costa Rica and other countries are an example of such success over time.

Buyer-driven value chain models

Buyer-driven models form the foundation for many of the applications of value chain financing. It is often in the buyer's interest to procure a flow of products and use finance as a way of facilitating and/or committing producers, processors and others in the chain to sell to them under specified conditions. Most often, when financing is involved, the conditions are binding through contracts. Whether these are formally registered or not, the agreements can still form the basis for loan recovery.

Contract farming is the most common buyer-driven value chain model. As the name suggests, it involves farm-level or farmer association-level contracts but these contracts usually originate from one or more levels further along the value chain. The contracts can be formalized in the legal system or can be informal, but binding agreements.

Agro-food chain coordination can be exercised in a number of ways, ranging from tight vertically integrated operations, with full ownership and control by a single firm, to more fragmented coordination arrangements, where there are no formal but rather ad hoc transactions between producers and their buyers. Contract farming is a modality of chain coordination whereby transactions between producers and other chain stakeholders are governed by pre-established agreements that can be more or less formal. Indeed, some forms of contract farming can even be seen as outsourced production, often called *outgrower schemes*, typically by an estate, processor, exporter or other chain agent, to a pool of producers. The contract (formal or informal farming agreement) may involve advancing inputs, funds and/or technical support, or it might be limited to product sales conditions, such as prices, quantities and delivery dates (Winn et al., 2009).

The interest in contract farming as a chain governance strategy has grown considerably in the recent past, probably because of the trends affecting agro-food systems, which are leading into more tightly aligned supply chains (da Silva, 2007). As a result, increased opportunities have emerged for contract farming arrangements to be promoted as conduits to leverage access to financial resources across agro-food supply chains.

Contract farming has some of the characteristics of a lead firm model, where a large processor, exporter or retailer provides buyer credit. However, contract farming often involves stricter terms that specify the type of production, quality, quantity and timing of agricultural product delivery. Finance and technical assistance provision, if needed, may be part of such an agreement. commitments between the farmer and buyer – whether contractual or verba provide bankers with a signal of security and seriousness, and a type of *delegated screening* described in Box 3.2 (Miller, 2007b). In fact, as a result of the existence of contracts, funding can be provided to farmers directly by an agribusiness firm or by a third party, such as a bank. In the first situation, agribusiness firms, such as agro-processors, will have their operational risks reduced, because access to raw materials is safeguarded by the contracts established with producers. This improves a firm's credit rating and allows it increased access to finance. The funds obtained by the firm are then channelled to farmers, often in the form of farming inputs and technical assistance. In the second case, since banks tend to consider producers to be more creditworthy if they have a guaranteed market for their products, the participation in a contractual relationship can serve as a form of virtual collateral. Acceptance or not of such collateral depends upon the lending organization and also upon the lending requirements of each country. However, in either case, contract farming is often an important mechanism supporting value chain financing.

Contracts may or may not be strictly formal. The Hortifruti case outlined in Box 3.2 below demonstrates the power of a verbal contract with a known

---

Box 3.2 Buyer relationship credit-worthiness, Costa Rica

Hortifruti is an institutional buyer that consolidates products from many different small-scale farmers who are its suppliers and sells the bulked produce to supermarkets. Although there is normally no formal contract between the farmer and the buyer, banks observe the relationship, and infer information about the farmer's credit-worthiness. This is a form of *delegated screening* of borrowers in which the informal contract linking the institutional buyer to the producer is the signal that tells the bank: go ahead and lend, because this is a good prospect. The bank has confirmation of the farmer's ability and willingness to repay based on the institutional buyer's need to work with efficient, responsible producers, and market risk is lessened by the guaranteed volume of sales obtained through the relationship with the institutional buyer. This same relationship reduces price risk and, because guaranteed sales to the supermarket chain are continuous all year long, it also protects the farmer from losses of liquidity. Thanks to a staggered planting and sales programme, based on instructions from the institutional buyer, farmers have liquidity throughout the year. With technical assistance, market information, and other non-financial services offered by the supermarket chain, farmers are able to mitigate productivity risks, environmental risks and quality problems that could lead to product rejection, while at the same time broadening their horizons, increasing investment and promoting innovation. A seemingly surprising note on Hortifruti suppliers is how heterogeneous they are and their most important distinguishing features are not easily visible. For example, producer size is relatively unimportant. In Costa Rica, the average farm size for Hortifruti suppliers is nine hectares. This is not a huge producer and others were even smaller. It was found that some farmers owned no land at all, but met their Hortifruti commitments on rented property. Even lacking land, they were able to find financial intermediaries willing to give them loans on the strength of nothing more than rented property and a contract and ongoing relationship with Hortifruti. They did not require land as collateral; a verbal contract with Hortifruti, an exceptionally strong and well-known company, was enough to make them creditworthy, at least for working capital financing.

Source: Quirós (2007: 45–65)

buyer, as a result of which farmers are able to access finance directly from a financial institution, even if they are raising crops on rented land.

Hortifruti also offers an example of a complex set of financing mechanisms that work together to support a value chain. The agreements between Hortifruti, farmers and processors enable the latter two to access finance from banking institutions.

Hortifruti also directly provides financing and/or guarantees in various other value chains as shown below in the case of rice and bean growers and processors. The table illustrates the structure and various types of finance that come into play in these chains.

Table 3.2 Hortifruti financing models

Bank financing for rice growers	Non-bank financing for rice and bean growers	Non-bank financing for rice and bean processors
1) *Hortifruti:* Guarantees purchase of crop under contract; contracts provide assurance to BAC San José bank for financing of rice growers.	1) *Hortifruti:* a) Guarantees purchase of crop under contract; contracts provide assurance to BAC bank for financing of rice growers. b) Finances farmers directly using company resources (30% of production cost); charges no interest (pays advance on purchase of the crop).	1) *Hortifruti:* Advances payment against future delivery of processed goods; buys industrial equipment of raw material.
2) *BAC San José:* Finances 60% of production costs; requires no collateral pledge; requires crop insurance policy.	2) Supply houses: Deliver inputs to farmer (agrochemicals, seeds, and small equipment).	2) Processor: Pays loan gradually by processing products; signed contract with Hortifruti provides access to credit; guaranteed stable, long-term commercial relationship.
3) *Processor:* Upon receipt and payment of rice, discounts farmer's debt to pay the bank and supply houses, with part of the value of the crop.	3) *Processor:* Upon receipt and payment of rice, discounts farmer's debt to pay the bank and supply houses, with part of the value of the crop.	3) *Farmer:* Signs pledge to deliver crop.
4) *Supply house:* Provides in-kind financing of 35% of the production costs, via inputs.	4) *Supply house:* Provides in-kind financing of 35% of the production costs, via inputs.	4) Working capital and inputs: Delivered to the farmer based on advance payment for crop.
5. *Farmer:* Signs pledge to deliver crop to rice mill; thus becomes more creditworthy with BAC San José.	5) *Farmer:* Signs pledge to deliver crop to rice mill; thus becomes more creditworthy with BAC San José.	

Source: adapted from Cavalini in Quirós (2007)

Thus, the Hortifruti-linked rice and bean producers avail of financing both *to* and *through* the value chain – to the chain from BAC San José with funds made possible because of their chain relationship and through the chain from both suppliers and Hortifruti.

In the many cases where contracts are more strictly formalized than the above example, they typically involve binding legal agreements that specify the roles and responsibilities of the producer and the buyer. On the production side, there are commonly terms regarding timing, volume, and quality of outputs. On the buyer side, commitments are made regarding inputs, technical assistance, purchasing and financing. A case from the Philippines (see Box 3.3) describes one such formal arrangement that channels funds from a bank through a processing firm to small-scale tomato farmers.

For financing, the benefit of contracts between producers/sellers and buyers is evident since contracts reduce uncertainty and risk of the unknown. However, before embracing buyer-driven models such as contract farming it is important to fully understand the models: What is the value to each party involved? What is the negotiating power and equity of each, especially between smallholders and large companies? What is the commitment and what is the risk of not honouring contracts, through side-selling (selling to others rather than the contracted party) or buyer refusal to buy under specified conditions, especially when market conditions change? Also, in what sectors are contract farming models most common and why?

Based upon its experiences with linkages and financing, Hortifruti is convinced that the contract farming model is a dynamic agent capable of promoting and facilitating social change in the agricultural sector of Central America. To take advantage of the model, Hortifruti recommends that 'the government, the NGO and companies work together to incorporate more producers in the countries of the region into the Hortifruti-type of business model and foster the concept of sustainability in production models used by small-scale farmers' (Cavalini in Quirós, 2007: 73–74). Yet, how does a model such as this go to scale with a large number of producers? From the examples presented at the four regional FAO conferences, it was clear that the experiences of contract farming have most often been with limited numbers of producers. One reason noted was that a majority of farmers are not ready to meet the requirements, hence the recommendation to governments and development organizations that they support producer capacity development – not only technical capacity but also organizational capacity and commitment.

In order to best understand the potential for increasing the use of contract farming as a model for facilitating financing it is useful to understand both the benefits and weaknesses.

Benefits and weaknesses of contract farming. Contract farming, whether formalized or informal, is a viable model to incorporate small-scale farmers into value chains and through the contractual arrangements enable them to access

Box 3.3 Formal contract agriculture, Philippines

Northern Foods Corporation (NFC), Philippines, is an agri-based firm which produces tomato paste and other agri-based products from indigenous crops. It received financing from the Rural Credit Guarantee Corporation (RCGC). NFC serves as an industrial link for small farmers who are contracted to produce tomatoes to be processed into tomato paste. The supply chain involves a Production Supply and Marketing Agreement between the NFC and tomato farmers, which guarantees NFC a continuous and adequate supply of fresh tomato for processing. To ensure quality of produce, the company provides input supplies and gives technical support to the farmers in accordance with Contract Growing Agreement. The tomatoes produced are then processed in compliance with Good Marketing Practices (GMP) and eventually distributed to various end users such as fish canners, processed sauce and ketchup manufacturers and major burger chains.

**NFC contract-linked
finance in the tomato chain**

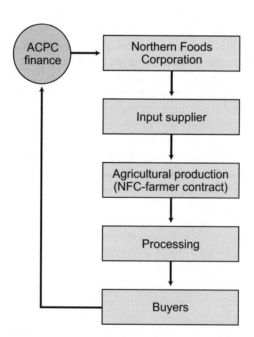

The implementation of this initiative brought out several benefits among the stakeholders within the value chain: 1) eliminated layers in the value chain since farmers are directly linked to the buyer/processors; 2) provided farmers with updated technical assistance, input supplies and protected floor prices; 3) reduced post-harvest spoilage since products are immediately forwarded to the buyers/processors; 4) assured supply of raw materials for processing; and 5) minimized dependency on imported tomato paste.

Source: Digal (2009)

credit and other services. Key among the many benefits and the challenges and risks of this system are:

Benefits:

- Access to secure markets and prices for producers.
- Access to appropriate input supplies in timely fashion.
- Increased access and reliability in procurement of product of desired quality for agribusiness buyers.
- Opportunity for lower input costs due to improved planning and economies of scale.
- Enhanced access to credit despite a lack of collateral.
- Support in the development and achievement of quality standards and certification.
- Provision of market-focused technical training and assistance that outlives contracts.
- Are often enforceable contracts which gives buyer a level of comfort.
- Potential advancement of positive relationships and increase in trust.

Challenges and risks:

- Reliance on a single buyer that could fail or lose interest in the relationship (loss of their buyer, market changes, bankruptcy).
- Side-selling by farmers, particularly if prices go up.
- Cost of management for buyer.
- Enforcement of contracts by either party.
- Regulatory environment for contracts and their enforcement.
- Tendency to favour larger farmers, at the expense of small farmers, due to lower transaction costs and a stronger initial asset base.
- Lack of technical capacity to understand and intentionally develop viable value chains, especially those involving small farmers.

In spite of the potential benefits to the participants of a contract farming agreement, not all contracting initiatives will be successful. The risks of failure are associated with a number of well-known reasons, chief of which is the opportunistic behaviour that might arise when pre-established conditions

---

Box 3.4 Failure of contract farming in tomato production in Brazil

In North-eastern Brazil a contracting initiative among agro-processors and tomato growers in a major agro-industrial project failed even though the companies pre-financed farmers with the provision of inputs and technical assistance. Although farmers had agreed on a pre-set price, during harvest time the market prices offered by traders in the region were so much higher that very few farmers fulfilled their delivery commitments, selling instead outside the contractual relationship and not repaying the companies for the pre-financed inputs and services. Because of this episode of contractual hold-up, the agro-processors decided to start importing concentrated tomato paste from Chile to meet their raw material needs, abandoning the contracting farming scheme.

Source: da Silva (2007)

change. If market prices rise above the agreed level and if alternative buyers exist for the agricultural products grown under the contract, then farmers might be enticed to renege on their contractual obligations and sell to the highest bidder as shown in Box 3.4.

Although not specifically documented, it is noted that contract farming has been most prevalent in sectors and market niches where side-selling is less of an option. This is the case, for instance, with sugar cane where the cost of a sugar mill and transport are so high there are few alternatives for side-selling by producers. The same can hold true for market niches, especially when the price premium is high compared to alternative markets. On the other hand, commodities such as maize with multiple producers and buyers and high price competition pose more risks of side-selling, hence the use of contract farming is not prevalent in these sectors.

Much can be done to help achieve the success factors indicated above. Development agencies can be instrumental in not only promoting capacity building and improved legislation, but in order to reduce risks in contract farming, they can support the building of transparent, equitable and well-functioning value chains. The form of risks will be different according to the context, and therefore risk mitigation strategies must adapt to fit the needs of the value chain and its stakeholders. As this facilitating role by implementing agencies is so important and growing in prevalence, it is treated as one of the business models for value chain development as described in the following section.

Box 3.5 Success factors for contract farming

Critical success factors for contract farming include the following:

- Mutual benefit for both parties – there must be a synergy, mutual trust and reciprocal dependency among partners.
- Creation of an enabling environment.
- Transaction costs and bottlenecks of dealing with multiple contracting parties must be minimized – this could be done by working with groups and BDS providers/facilitators.
- Appropriate consideration of production and marketing risks in the design of contracts.
- Careful selection of enterprise – high value, processing and exports-related enterprises have shown most success.
- For micro- and small-scale producers to be financed efficiently, transparent partnerships among stakeholders with a shared interest are important.
- Clear quality standards which must be understood at all levels – e.g. farmers need to understand what is expected of them beforehand, and not after their crops are already half-grown.
- Mechanisms for providing fast, direct or rapid financing to the micro- and small-scale businesses in the chain when necessary.

Source: adapted from da Silva (2007)

Facilitated value chain models

In many countries there is almost a dual agricultural system in which a developed agro-industry coexists alongside marginalized producers who are living at subsistence levels. Facilitation by development organizations, both NGOs and government agencies, has demonstrated that external support can open up opportunities for smallholder value chain integration and financing.

Larger buyers and wholesale chains often seek out large-scale suppliers due to a number of factors that are challenging when dealing with small-scale farmers who:

- May not be well organized.
- Have not demonstrated commitment.
- Require higher transaction costs to be served.
- Often pose increased risks such as side-selling.
- Lack both technical capacity and the technologies to reliably produce the high quality and quantity required in a consistent manner.
- Tend to lack organizational capacity and resources to deliver the required products in a timely fashion.

Consequently, the costs of organizing and training small producers can be deemed too high to be taken on by a large company.

Development agencies and others with a social mission can provide support to facilitate the integration of small famers and agro-enterprises into commercial value chains. Successful facilitation models for value chain development have been developed around the world. With proper organization and training, incomes can be improved, for example:

> In Uganda, ARUDESI has been able to work with 8,000 farmers to organize 600 farmer groups consisting of 30 farmers per group. These farmers were able to market a total of 1,200 metric tonnes of green coffee in the last 3 years, increasing income of an average of 40 per cent over equivalent green coffee at farm gate price. (Mrema, 2007)

Many contract farming or other value chain linkage models which involve small producers are able to thrive in part due to the facilitation and/or services provided or initiated by not-for-profit or government agencies. In some cases, the agencies facilitate relationships including those between producers and financial institutions. In others, the agencies themselves enter into contractual arrangements (including guarantees), and provide direct technical services and finance. TechnoServe, a not-for-profit development agency that works in agricultural value chains around the world, demonstrates how an external agency, acting as a market developer, can facilitate the development of a chain through interventions at various levels. See Box 3.6.

A guiding principle of TechnoServe facilitation in all of their development activities is to incorporate a private sector focused business model as a means of building sustainability. In financing, this involves such things as direct involvement of banks, commercial investors and private equity funds for asset finance needs. For working capital needs, financing from banks and buyers can be available if there is customized technical assistance. This is especially the case for start-ups and early stage expansion of agribusinesses.

Box 3.6 Facilitating chain development in Malawi and Tanzania

TechnoServe utilizes various business models to enhance smallholder incomes through processing business, supply business and out-grower models. In Malawi, TechnoServe is facilitating the seed industry value chain in response to severe financing gaps in agribusiness in southern Africa which is characterized by asset finance needs and working capital needs. The reasons for a lack of access to finance, especially by start-up seed businesses and early stage expansions, have mainly been shortage of risk capital and poor business management capacity. TechnoServe developed the following three-pronged business model to address the needs in the seed chain:

- Processing businesses – facilitating enhanced value addition and farmer linkages.
- Input supply businesses – facilitating improved seed, access to fertilizer and production technology.
- Farmer businesses – facilitating farmer integration into the seed production, processing and marketing chain through farmer organization, training and out-grower contracts.

By addressing the whole chain, TechnoServe is able to secure a market for the fledgling seed businesses and a more secure repayment of the financing, while stimulating income growth and development of the small producers. This approach for assisting small farmers is summed up in TechnoServe's strategy to:

- Support a service provider to provide marketing and financial linkages to farmer groups.
- Identify and organize farmer groups with potential to produce quality.
- Assist groups to invest in improving quality and production.

Kilicafe in Tanzania, an organization TechnoServe helped create that is now owned by 9,000 smallholder farmers, works with local and international financial institutions to design financial products that serve those in the value chain. These products range from short-term input credit and sales pre-financing to multi-year loans used by farmers to invest in centralized processing facilities. Credit is guaranteed through a variety of innovative means, including private guarantee funds, warehouse receipts and forward sales to specialty coffee buyers. These included:

- Long-term financing for processing infrastructure, secured by fixed assets and marketing agreements.
- Short-term financing for working capital, advance payments to farmers and agro-input credit, secured by guarantee funds, warehouse receipts, marketing agreements and price risk management.

However, initially the local banks did not understand the business model, the risks, nor accept coffee as full collateral. The financial arrangements built according to the value chain were only possible due to significant initial support from TechnoServe to both the banks and the clients, developing business plans, monitoring performance and ongoing operational assistance, until credit-worthiness was fully established.

Source: S. Harris presentation in Kimathi et al. (2007)

In western Kenya, DrumNet provides an example of an innovative, multi-stakeholder facilitated value chain which links together farmers, input suppliers, buyers and banks through a fee-based facilitator hub that is coordinated through cell phone text messages. As facilitator, DrumNet provides the organization and capacity building of the farmers' associations as well as the relationship and Internet linkages between the various parties involved (Campaigne, 2007). For further illustration, a DrumNet sunflower sector case study (see Case Study 4) is presented in detail at the end of chapter five.

In addition to capacity building, successful facilitator models include three key aspects as highlighted by Odo (2007) from his vast experience in the field of farmer organization and agricultural chain development. He states:

- Start with the market and work backwards.
- Aggregate producers and their goods.
- Use the value chain for obtaining finance, such as buyer credit secured by sales contracts.

A word of caution on facilitation is given by Marangu (2007) who notes that since value chains are dynamic and complex, a facilitator must carefully prioritize interventions at key leverage points throughout the chain. Moreover, facilitators must stay out of the supply chain and avoid direct provision of financial services or subsidizing the cost of business. Such actions distort commercial signals.

Facilitation models can be proactive in identifying and developing value chains. For example, USAID's technical assistance via the Peru Poverty Reduction Assistance (PRA) project identifies and facilitates value chain opportunities such as artichoke cultivation for small farmers in the highlands of Peru (see Box 3.7). PRA identified market opportunities, provided information, and brought together producers, processors and buyers to meet the needs of the market. Worldwide demand for processed artichokes has more than doubled over the past 20 years. Peru has been trying to capture part of the large European market and is well positioned to do so, given its labour cost advantages.

Figure 3.2 represents the value chain for Peruvian artichokes described in Box 3.7. Arrows in the diagram indicate the direction of financial flows in the value chain and the role of the formal financial system in financing the chain (Campion, 2006).

As noted above, financing is both to and through the value chain for the export artichokes. In the less structured local wholesale market and supermarkets there were no financial flows within the chain. In the artichoke value chain, inputs, secured markets, financing, as well as technical assistance were all important ingredients – a complete service package – that enabled smallholder farmers to enter the market. Finance alone will rarely result in increased quality and sales.

With small producers, technical assistance and knowledge is often missing on how to invest in a way that will increase production of high quality products and command higher prices. By addressing this issue and with the demonstrated success with artichokes, the sources of finance expanded from financing from within the chain by suppliers and buyers to access from financial institutions for those producers.

A pending issue to resolve on value chain facilitation is that of sustainability and payment of services, especially when dealing with small producers and processors. It appears that the private sector is not willing and/or able to take full responsibility for building this capacity. Is the required facilitation support a public good, as are many of the universities in developing countries that will require support from the government and development organizations?

Box 3.7 Facilitating artichoke chain development and finance in Peru

The retail market for artichoke is outside Peru, in the United States and Europe, making it difficult for small farmers without facilitation support. Otherwise, representatives of wholesalers who operate in Peru work directly with processors and prefer to work with a small number of large companies rather than many small ones, so as to assure a steady supply. They offer a contract specifying the exact price they will pay for the largest volume of processed artichokes their suppliers can produce. Because processors have a contract and a fixed price, they know exactly how much they can pay farmers for the product. Much like wholesalers, they also would prefer to work with a few larger producers, but because most of the land is divided into small parcels, processors generally must buy from small farmers.

To improve the chain and facilitate its access to small farmers, the USAID funded project identified the market opportunity and then worked with Agromantaro – a processor – to encourage it to begin artichoke processing. Subsequently, the main focus was working with local community organizations to encourage small producers to grow artichokes and assist in facilitating external financing.

Since artichokes are a new crop which is unfamiliar and perceived to be risky, processors go to the producer organizations to help convince small farmers to produce for them. For this purpose, they offer:

(a) a contract; (b) a fixed price; (c) seedlings; (d) technical assistance.

The need for seedlings and technical assistance was to minimize production risks. Farmers do not pay for seedlings until harvest, so in this sense, the processor is involved in financing the crop. Fertilizer companies supply farmers by selling to independent distributors and offering them volume discounts and commercial credit, just as they do with the large producers. The distributors then extend commercial credit to the farmers for repayment a few months later when the harvest comes in. They also provide free technical assistance on optimizing the use of inputs, which in turn reduces the risk of default.

Typically in Peru, very little formal credit goes to agriculture. However, when word got out that this chain was working well, non-banking financial institutions began to take an interest. In particular rural and municipal credit unions and the Edpyme Confianza started to offer direct loans to small farmers, thus releasing processors to use their capital for expanding their own investments.

Source: Campion in Quirós (2007)

Integrated value chain models

The fourth business model is the integrated value chain model. It not only connects producers to others in the chain – input suppliers, intermediaries, processors, retailers and service providers including finance – but it integrates many of these through ownership and/or formal contractual relationships. The integrated model has many of the features of the other models presented such as strong links with multi-party arrangements, technical guidance and strict compliance, and also incorporates an amalgamated structure of value chain flows and services.

The first and most common integrated model involves vertical integration within the value chain. Integration is normally sought by a large retailer or wholesaler/importer that is focused on consumer demand, and wishes to ensure that inputs, production and post-harvest handling will result in products that are responsive to that demand. The degree of overall vertical (and often

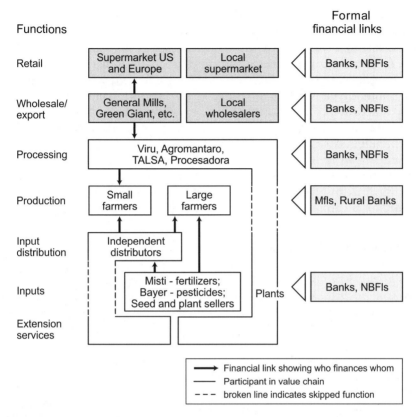

Figure 3.2 Artichoke value chain
Source: Campion (2006)

horizontal) integration in the model depends upon the degree to which the individual levels are tightly linked – from control of production through to retail – often by means of contract farming or other contractual buyer models. Vertically integrated supermarket value chains are a prime example of this model. A supermarket works closely with importers or domestic wholesalers in order to convey information about acceptable product specifications such as variety, quality, volume, and standards relating to hygiene, traceability and residues. Information and services are passed down the chain to producers, frequently accompanied by quality control, technical training, appropriate inputs, record keeping and finance. Such vertical integration particularly applies to fresh fruits and vegetables. Horticultural value chains can be excellent for the integration of smallholder farmers since, for many of the products, intensive labour and manual cultivation and harvesting are necessary to deliver the required output.

Coffee is a specific agricultural output that often involves vertical integration – not the lower quality Robusta varieties that are subjected to extensive processing to achieve its final form, but finer Arabica coffee that relies on inputs, climatic conditions and cultivation techniques. Starbucks Coffee Company, described later in Box 4.7, offers a model of tight integration from production to retail.

A second integrated model applied to value chains is that of an integrated services model. One type of services model is led by a financial conglomerate and another type is led by a facilitating entity which combines ownership structures with their facilitation. The latter type could be led by a strong NGO, such as BRAC in Bangladesh as described in Box 3.8, or an agribusiness services centre such as are being developed in India.

BRAC offers an important example as a financial institution that makes direct strategic investments in the chain when it sees the financing of its clients requires this. For example, BRAC set up and owned chicken hatcheries needed for poultry production of its clients. It also offers the required techni-

---

Box 3.8 BRAC integrated services model for agriculture, Bangladesh

BRAC, a national, private organization, started as an almost entirely donor funded, small scale relief and rehabilitation project, and evolved into an independent, virtually self-financed organization in sustainable human development. Currently the largest NGO in the world, BRAC employees number more than 100,000 who work with the twin objectives of poverty alleviation and empowerment of the poor. At the centre of the BRAC approach are over 170,000 village organisations (VOs), each with 30–40 mostly women members, which are set up to provide social support and microfinance services. These village organisations meet weekly to receive training, distribute loans, collect repayments and savings contributions, and raise awareness on many social, legal and personal issues affecting the everyday lives of poor women.

Building on this model, BRAC supports a number of programmes including agribusiness. The objective of this approach is to promote agribusiness activities to generate employment and help alleviate poverty. Specially, it (i) promotes small scale agribusiness activities by channelling credit through three NGOs including BRAC and by providing technical and marketing support to small scale agribusiness throughout the rural areas of the country to raise the level of value addition and increase rural incomes; (ii) strengthen participating NGOs and wholesale banks to ensure efficiency of the credit implementation and management; (iii) strengthen agribusiness associations for policy dialogue on the enabling environment, agribusiness promotion and information dissemination. BRAC also becomes directly engaged in businesses which needed to support of rural enterprises engaged in commercial agriculture production, input supply, marketing, processing and transportation. As an example, BRAC businesses include: 6 poultry farms for supplying day-old chicks, 3 feed mills, 2 seed production centres, 2 seed processing centres, 15 nurseries and 12 fish or prawn hatcheries also with the purpose of strengthening the respective value chains. Together, its business model works to ensure an integrated set of services for its clients.

Key issues in agricultural activities for BRAC are:

- creation of basic awareness and provision of training to farmers;
- development of village-based technical service providers;
- adequate supply of quality inputs through extension workers/agents;
- assurance of market access of farmers;
- provision of appropriate loan packages for farmers to meet their specific demands;
- development of linkages among different value chains.

Source: Salenque (2007)

cal assistance and can facilitate marketing channels as needed. It has also done this for the artisan craft sector, including wholesale and retail of the crafts. Through financial services and strategic investments directly into the value chain, it generates employment in rural and peri-urban areas and raises the value added of the produce of its clients.

While not widespread, integrated agricultural value chain service models are growing in importance. Case Study 3 on LAFISE in Latin America, presented at the end of Chapter 4, describes a commercial integrated banking and agricultural service model. A Rabobank example from India is also being adapted and used to fit into countries in many parts of the world.

As noted in Figure 3.3, Rabobank assumes a central role in the value chain providing financial and value chain support services throughout the chain. By having such a central role as part of its business model, it knows the business sector and those involved. In this way, it can ensure that the linkages are efficient and that any weaknesses among the partners are addressed so as not to cause problems to others in the chain. Since the money also passes through the bank, it can reduce costs by directly crediting and debiting the accounts of those in the value chain.

Credit advances from marketing or processor businesses are often related specifically to a single value chain since most companies, especially private ones, work in only one or a few value chains. However, they can exist within a complex system of interrelated agribusiness services which offer financial and non-financial services of a comprehensive nature for multiple value chains. In Korea, one agricultural entity, formed under a cooperative structure, has a huge presence in the whole agricultural sector which allows it to provide integrated value chain services in multiple value chains as in the case shown in Box 3.9.

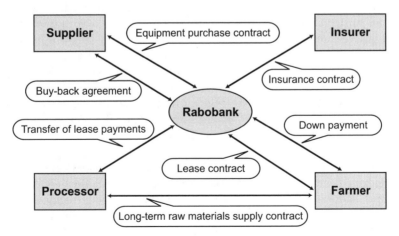

Figure 3.3 Rabobank integrated agriculture finance structure
Source: Wortelboer (2007)

Box 3.9 National Agricultural Cooperative Federation, Korea

The Republic of Korea has been experiencing significant growth in major industries, including agriculture. The National Agricultural Cooperative Federation (NACF) has played a decisive role in the development of the country's agricultural industry. NACF is a national federation of 1,187 agricultural cooperatives in Korea. The Federation and its member cooperatives offer multifunctional services to its 2.4 million individual members. These include: 1) banking and insurance; 2) input supply; 3) agricultural marketing and livestock; and 4) guidance and welfare services. Within the banking and insurance services, the Federation and its member cooperatives are connected with each other for mobilizing and providing the agricultural finance services for farmers and agri-industries throughout the country.

The cooperative structure of NACF in Korea lends itself to perform an integrated, full-service model of agricultural and non-agricultural services which benefit its members. Its size allows NACF to operate across multiple chains and benefit from the synergies of services and inputs across these chains. The NACF has 22 subsidiary companies to help provide these services, which include four other agricultural marketing companies besides the parent company NACF, a logistics service company and the Nonghyup Economic Research Institute. It provides commercial finance, mutual finance, loan guarantees and insurance and other services through other subsidiaries including: 1) Namhae Chemical Corporation; 2) Korea Agricultural Marketing, Inc.; 3) Korea Agricultural Cooperative Trading, Ltd.; 4) NACF Futures Corporation; 5) Korea Coop-Agro, Inc.; 6) Nonghyup Korea Ginseng Co.; 7) Nonghyup Feed, Inc.; 8) Nonghyup CA Asset management Co., Ltd.; 9) Agricultural Cooperative Asset Management Co., Ltd.; and 10) NH Investment & Securities. It also provides social support through subsidiaries including: 1) Nonghyup Tours; 2) Agricultural Cooperative College; and 3) The Farmers Newspaper. In combination, the NACF and its subsidiaries represent an integrated model which is capable of providing virtually all agricultural value chain services needed by its members.

Source: Park (2007) and author's personal correspondence with C. Choi (2009)

The NACF model in Korea and the cooperative banking model of Rabobank are both successful models. Whereas Rabobank focuses on the integration of financial services along the chain and linkages with the chain partners, NACF also can participate directly in the chain. In other words, the multiple value chain services are different from those of Rabobank in that NACF itself acts as supplier, insurer, processor, and marketer for its member farmers and not only as a financial services provider. For example, farmers can purchase their farm machines from NACF with NACF loans guaranteed by the agricultural guarantee fund, and they can sell their products to NACF operating markets through their local cooperatives. In the same manner, the farmers' money is transferred to their NACF savings account, and later the money can be used towards repaying their loans.

Private, non-cooperative models and in some cases integrated governmental models have been demonstrated to be successful. However, they are complex and much caution must be noted – their success often depends highly upon the superb management capacity and the social and economic environment within which they were formed. More often than not, these conditions are not present. For example, in Eastern Europe and Central Asia large integrated agricultural value chains, with embedded financing, were also formed and were not sustainable over time (Winn, 2009). In Kenya, as noted earlier, the large integrated model of the Agricultural Finance Corporation together with the Kenya Farmers Association and the National Cereals Produce Board also failed.

Introduction to Case Study

As described in this chapter, a value chain business model can be a sophisticated, integrated model with a large bank in the centre, a bottom-up producer driven model or one which is buyer driven. What is important is to have a clear, business model which is competitive and is built upon a strong foundation. For this reason business models involving small producers within the value chain often receive governmental or non-governmental development support in building the capacity and facilitating linkages to fully integrate them into strong value chains.

The following case study from Kenya describes the experience of a development organization in facilitating the building of an inclusive value chain and creating a strong foundation for long-term success of smallholder farmers.

Case Study 1. Farm Concern International: commercial village approach

Grace Ruto, Programme Administrator, Farm Concern International

'Enhancing market access for African traditional vegetables' was designed against the back drop of emerging consumer demand for African traditional vegetables. Supported by the Rockefeller Foundation, Gatsby UK, Farm Africa and IPGRI (now Bioversity International) and implemented in Kenya and Tanzania by Farm Concern International (FCI) and the World Vegetable Centre (AVRDC), the project sought to empower small-scale women farmers through sustainable leafy vegetable production, seed supply and marketing of high quality African traditional vegetables (ATV) in Eastern Africa.

The project focused on enhanced ATV commercialization, productivity skills for smallholders, increased utilization to streamline efficiency of the value chains, consumption linkages and improvement of health, nutrition and income of vulnerable groups. It sought to stimulate home gardening and commercial farming systems with a focus on progressive economic development and enterprise promotion related to the mainstream activities of the target groups and the needs of smallholder producers in Kenya.

The ATV project implementation was based on Farm Concern International's successful approach to smallholder commercialization – the Commercial Village Approach (CVA)® – a model tested across various villages and a diversity of smallholder commodities. Under the CVA, a four-pronged strategic approach for the project was designed which included: 1) ATV commercialization;

2) smallholder seed multiplication systems; 3) value chain development; and 4) market development and demand creation.

At the start of the project in 2003, a baseline survey was undertaken by FCI and AVRDC to assess ATV production and marketing status. The baseline revealed no ATV commercialization in the target regions and neighbouring areas, weak seed supply systems and minimal ATV awareness among target farmers. The Nairobi market was transacting approximately 31 tonnes of ATVs per month primarily sourced from western Kenya and transported in burlap bags to Nairobi via night buses. By 2006 the ATV seed system was benefiting 300 smallholder women farmers in western Kenya while over 2,700 small-holder farmers are currently practicing ATV commercial farming in the central region of Kiambu. Consumption for ATV in Nairobi increased from 31 tonnes in 2003, with an estimated farm-gate value of US$ 6,000, to 600 tonnes in 2006, with a value of US$ 142,860 and farm-gate prices have increased by 30 per cent. The supply of 500 tonnes in 2007 is estimated to account for 60 per cent of the demand level within the ATV distribution network that includes supermarkets, kiosks, informal markets and street markets.

Market access financing

Effective partnerships with smallholder farmers required a wide range of business development services (BDS) like transport and credit to ensure timely supply. However, farmers lacked resources to invest in the required BDS which prompted FCI to develop partnerships between farmers and various BDS providers focused on leveraging resources from private sector players.

Uchumi Supermarkets, like many formal markets, procures produce on a 30–60 days credit period which smallholder farmers could not sustain due to limited resources. In order to commence a sustainable approach that would maintain smallholder farmers in the marketplace, FCI injected a fund of approximately US$ 100,000 – a Market Access Financial Service (MacFin) – aimed at discounting the credit period and settling transport bills while the fund was gradually recovered from Uchumi payments. To enhance the producer groups to build and maintain a fund similar to MacFin, FCI introduced a savings component where the groups commenced with 10 per cent savings. This has enabled some groups to be weaned off the FCI MacFin and discount invoices from a group-managed fund. Producer groups weaned off MacFin have further attracted microfinance institutions (MFIs) due to their savings, enabling them to access credit for ATV commercial expansion.

MacFin, the fund created by FCI to increase smallholders' participation along value chains has the following unique characteristics:

1. It is a catalytic fund and only accessible to producer groups over a certain period (3–4 years).
2. It is utilized for transactional costs for assured markets, e.g. transport, packaging materials, invoice discounting, inputs, etc.

3. It is accessed only by collective marketing groups.
4. It requires group savings conducted over the period of time a group is accessing MacFin.
5. ATV collective marketing groups receive 10 per cent per sale.
6. The group leadership structure follows that recommended by FCI.
7. Group constitutions are developed to suit the particular functions of the group.

The MacFin programme and the MacFin catalytic fund provide support and facilitation to the 'bottom of the pyramid' community members, most of whom

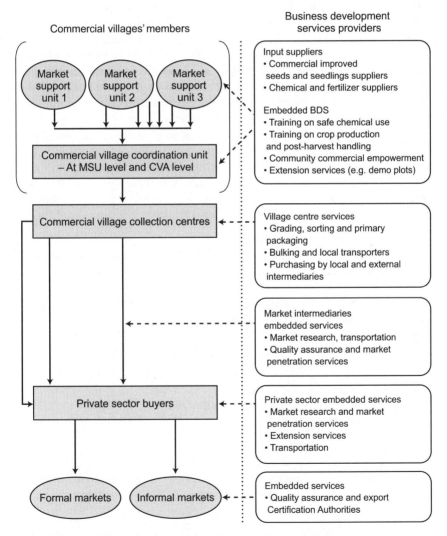

Figure 3.4 Commercial village approach for African traditional vegetables
Source: Farm Concern International (2008)

are not creditworthy, in order to trigger commercialization of community opportunities through enhanced market access and improved competitiveness. In the last two years MacFin has helped the Kiambu farmers in enhanced access to inputs, credit for marketing, as well as in meeting BDS costs like transport and invoice discounting of credit. The credit is advanced at 1 per cent per month interest and subsequently recovered from the formal and semi-formal sales.

For enhanced commercialization and bulking, FCI applies the CVA model illustrated in Figure 3.4 through which villages are commercialized and strategically linked to markets. This model, developed by FCI offers a village platform to achieve increased participation of smallholders into the mainstream marketing systems through financial and marketing interventions.

The MacFin fund has enabled the Kiambu Commercial Villages to pay the transaction costs which include transportation as well as purchase of inputs for specified range of ATVs. Upon selling their products to identified institutional buyers' farmers are paid promptly as part of FCI effort to cushion farmers' against long credit periods which could push them out of business. Farm Concern International would then recover advanced monies upon maturing of corresponding invoice.

During this period the project has managed to mobilize and establish partnership with targeted value chain players and has helped the farmers with better access to inputs, credit for marketing as well as in meeting BDS costs like transport and invoice discounting of credit. In summary, the rollout has progressively persuaded the key project partners to take up roles outlined as follows:

Farm Concern International
- community mobilization and establishment of commercial villages;
- development of ATV value networks;
- assist commercial villages access inputs;
- promote and strengthen savings and credit schemes;
- private sector partnership establishment;
- market access and development for commercial villages;
- community capacity building and extension support.

Agro-dealers
- offer credit to value chain players;
- offer technical back stopping on best agronomic practices.

Commercial village members
- procure seeds from identified agro-dealers;
- engage in commercial production of ATVs;
- service authentic orders from identified buyers in a timely manner;
- collectively bulk and market ATVs.

CV Executive committee
- coordinate and oversee the functions of respective market support units (MSU);

- organize production and supply schedule;
- encourage CVA to collectively bulk and market ATVs;
- collate, verify and approve input orders for MSU;
- ensure group saving;
- be co-guarantors to MSUs.

Microfinance Institutions
- offer credit to value chain players;
- offer technical back-stopping on credit management.

Farmer base

At the onset of the project four sites were selected for commercial villages' establishment namely, Githiga, Lower Lari, Kahuho and Karura. The programme has a current farmer base of 2,113 smallholder farmers distributed over 4 commercial villages, with 72 groups having an average of 30 members per producer group otherwise referred to as MSUs. The intervention was received with enthusiasm leading to a notable increase in client base by up to 120 per cent in the first 6 months. All the MSUs are registered with the Ministry of Culture and Social Services and operate group bank accounts. Individual members were also encouraged to operate personal saving accounts and, as a result, up to 50 per cent currently own and operate personal savings accounts. All the groups are governed through elected subcommittees and one executive committee and have developed group as well as commercial village constitutions.

Collective marketing structures

Each CVA group has an average of 30 members and each is structured as a complete management group with an executive leadership team of five (a chairperson, vice-chairperson, treasurer, secretary and assistant secretary). Under the executive leadership team are four other subcommittees – production, marketing, finance and welfare. The structure ensures an elaborate feedback process whereby, all subcommittees report to the executive committee through the representative of the subcommittee who sits in it. The executive committee ensures that the subcommittees are well run and are able to handle the group matters that relate to them.

Seed credit: 'Mkopo wa mbegu' scheme

Under the seed credit scheme the commercial villages have been assisted in accessing ATV seeds through identified agro-dealers. The commercial village members usually generate a seed request list which is verified and approved by the commercial village executive committee. The request is then forwarded to FCI's credit officer who prepares a purchase order in favour of a pre-approved agro-dealer. Upon presentation of the approved purchase order to the relevant agro-dealer, the commercial village representative is accordingly issued with ATV seeds as per the order. Thereafter, the agro-dealer presents to FCI a weekly invoice for seeds issued to farmers and is paid promptly. A transaction charge of 1 per cent is charged on the credit advanced. Commercial village members co-guarantee one another. Over 90 per cent of the target farmers in the programme have benefited from the scheme and have dedicated a portion of their land to production of ATVs. The advanced amount is recovered from sales realized within the season.

Figure 3.5 illustrates highlights of the market access financing intervention.

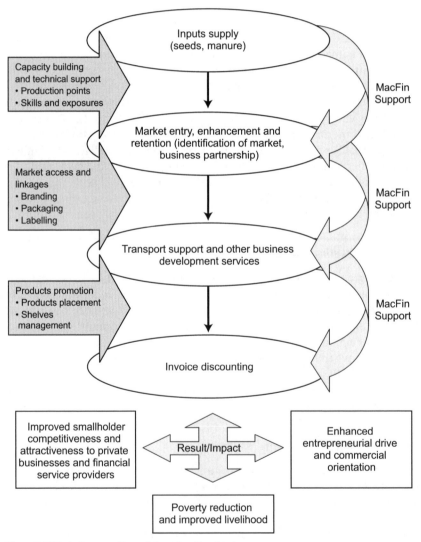

Figure 3.5 Market access financial service flowchart
Source: Farm Concern International (2008)

Invoice discounting: Mkopo wa soko scheme

This financial service has been offered to the commercial villages to enable farmers to access formal markets and at the same time help cushion them against long periods without funds which could push them out of business. Through this scheme about 400 new farmers have been able to access formal markets and consistently service their orders. The fund has bolstered their cash flow ensuring that they have sufficient funds to plough back into their farming business, thus enabling them to save sufficient funds to cover other market related expenses like transport and communication.

Portfolio

The average outstanding loan portfolio per commercial village is US$388. Members repay their loans flexibly based on available cash flows which correspond to their ATV sales. The portfolio risk has been greatly reduced by tying credit advanced to mandatory sales to identified markets, thus guaranteeing full repayment within 90 days.

Employment creation

Most of the farmers rely solely on family labour from production to the market. This is mainly due to the small acreage under production and by the fact that ATV production is not labour intensive.

Increased savings

Group savings and credit facilities have been established and strengthened through training and the establishment of financial coordinating committees at the MSU and commercial village levels, linkages to financial services providers and establishment of MacFin services. All MSUs are encouraged to establish

Table 3.3 Sales in target sites (March–August, 2008)

Commercial village	Benefiting members	Sales (Kshs)	Sales (US$)	Target market
Fresh vegetables				
Kiambu	381	7,335,309	104,790	Formal markets
Kiambu	736	14,221,707	203,167	Informal markets
Sub-total	–	21,557,016	307,957	
ATV seeds				
Kiambu	361	180,320	2,576	Local markets
Kiambu	612	169,300	2,418	Agro dealers
Sub-total	–	349,620	4,994	
Cumulative sales		21,903,636	312,951	

Source: Farm Concern International (2008)

saving mechanisms through operating bank accounts as a MSU and saving at least 10 per cent of their incomes generated from sales of vegetables. The records are kept by the financial subcommittees. Sixty per cent of the groups have complied with the savings recommendation and some groups have strived to save up to 15 per cent of sales realized. Several fora have been held with financial institutions in order to expose the farmers to a range of products offered. Field days have also been organized to allow farmers to exchange ideas with others farmers who have participated in the credit schemes.

Linkage to banks and microfinance institutions

A number of bank and microfinance institutions were identified by farmers and FCI for partnership with the commercial villages – KADET Ltd, Faulu Kenya, Family Bank, Cooperative Bank, Equity Bank, ECLOF and Unity Finance. A business partnership forum between commercial village leaders, a bank representative, a savings and credit co-operative organization (SACCO) representative and a FCI representative, was held with a view to establishing partnership agreements. Negotiations on terms of agreement are conducted through these fora. Eighty percent of the MSUs were exposed to financial institutions through scheduled meetings and a field day was organized which personalized interactions between financial service providers and farmers. Individual farmers have conversely been linked to MFIs with over 200 farmers already accessing credit from Family Bank, Unity Finance and Kagwe Tea SACCO.

Challenges encountered:
- The 2007 election campaign followed by post-election turmoil interfered with project rollout in January and February 2008.
- Disrupted ATVs marketing value chain in Kiambu site and Nairobi, due to the post-election turmoil and increased cost of transportation from farm-gate to the markets, threatened to erode group savings.
- The rising costs of farm inputs, especially manure and fertilizer, have marginally impeded ATVs commercialization among mobilized farmers.
- Inflation has also pushed up financial institutions' base lending rates hence making credit costly and less attractive to "bottom of the pyramid" communities.
- The intervention generated a lot of interest leading to high demand for the financial service, thus overstretching the current fund allocation.

Lessons learnt:
- It was noted that benefits to producer groups were realized through market awareness of ATVs along the value chain once collective action had been adopted. Collective action at production level resulted in cost reduction through bulking of farm produce and shared transport costs which attracted private players.

- It was also noted that communities at the bottom of the pyramid require financial services tailored to their needs. Such financial products could easily be adopted by the communities through demonstration of the interventions' performance at farm level and market level. This would be more effective if specific households successfully benefiting from the product are used as case studies in reaching out to other farmers.

Conclusions

Market-led, pro-poor market development. Smallholder-based market development requires an increased identification of products presenting a high-to-intermediate demand growth, offering the poor an opportunity to retain a market share. Medium and large-scale farmers are noticed to 'push' smallholders out of the market; however, to sustain smallholders in business the approach ought to further integrate the identification of products offering smallholders a competitive advantage e.g. ATV low cost of production is suitable for smallholders who primarily use animal manure from their small-scale farms.

Role of collective action in market development for smallholders. Collective action plays a vital role in increasing the participation of the poor in the marketplace. However skills on strategic collective market entry are required to ensure a sustained market entry, consistent market information feedback and partnerships with private value chain players. Farmers organized into MSUs have successfully adopted professional business skills that enhance their voices along value chains and in the marketplace.

Financial services embedded to market linkages. Smallholder farmers are still highly disadvantaged by the existing mode of savings and credit which hinders the access to credit for seasonal income earners. However, the FCI approach of embedding financial services to market linkages through the MacFin model has proven that credit as a stand alone product may not necessarily increase income, but credit embedded into market access increases rural income and contributes to increased rural savings and reduced poverty levels.

Case references

Morimoto, Y. and Maundu, P. (2006) *Rediscovering a Forgotten Treasure*, International Plant Genetics Resource Institute (IPGRI), Rome.
Mumbi, K., Karanja, N., Njenga, M., Kamore, M., Achieng, C., and Ngeli, P. (2006) *Viable Market Opportunities and Threats for Urban and Peri-Urban Farmers*, Farm Concern International, Urban Harvest and International Potato Center, Nairobi.

CHAPTER 4
Agricultural value chain finance instruments

Product overview

There are many ways to categorize the modalities, and describe the various financial products and tools that can be used. Wenner (2006), for example, states that the main modalities of value chain financing are: trade finance, secured transactions, risk management and financial enhancement instruments. Here we have chosen to organize the modalities differently, according to the analysis of the practical application of the various mechanisms described in greater detail here. Therefore, this chapter organizes instruments by product financing, receivables financing, physical asset collateralization, risk mitigation and structured enhancements, and provides illustrated descriptions of the most common products.

It must further be noted that the use of terms vary somewhat between countries and even across sectors. In some contexts, a precise legal term may be applied, but the use of the terms in agriculture may often encompass a broader meaning and application. This broader application is used in the descriptions that follow.

Table 4.1 provides a summary overview of value chain finance instruments – both traditional forms of credit as well as more sophisticated and complex models that are being implemented in today's environment of more tightly integrated value chains and financial systems. Not all of these instruments are applicable to small farmers' suppliers or traders – many risk management tools, for example, are more practical for agro-industries and wholesalers. However, these 'higher level' tools can stabilize prices, reduce risks and/or reduce the cost of financing, with the benefits passing to participants throughout the value chain.

Product financing

Trade-related financing is the most frequently used form of value chain finance. These credits most often assume the form of either: 1) 'pre-financed sales' when credit is provided to farmers by vendors who sell farm inputs, or 2) 'advance payments' given by buyers who purchase farm outputs. Various forms and instruments of product financing have been used for centuries and are often in-kind credit, such as in the form of seeds and fertilizer.

The product financing instruments described in the following sections are not new; rather, what is noteworthy is the way an agricultural value chain

Table 4.1 Description of agricultural value chain finance instruments

Instrument	Brief description
A. Product financing	
1. Trader credit	Traders advance funds to producers to be repaid, usually in kind, at harvest time. This allows traders to procure products, and provides a farmer with needed cash (for farm or livelihood usage) as well as a guaranteed sale of outputs. Less commonly, trader finance can also be used 'upward' in the chain whereby the trader delivers products to buyers with delayed payments.
2. Input supplier credit	An input supplier advances agricultural inputs to farmers (or others in the VC) for repayment at harvest or other agreed time. The cost of credit (interest) is generally embedded into the price. Input supplier credit enables farmers to access needed inputs while increasing sales of suppliers.
3. Marketing company credit	A marketing company, processor or other company provides credit in cash or in kind to farmers, local traders or other value chain enterprises. Repayment is most often in kind. Upstream buyers are able to procure outputs and lock in purchase prices and in exchange farmers and others in the value chain receive access to credit and supplies and secure a market for selling their products.
4. Lead firm financing	A lead firm either provides direct finance to value chain enterprises including farmers, or guaranteed sales agreements enabling access to finance from third party institutions. Lead firm financing, often in the form of contract farming with a buy-back clause, provides farmers with finance, technical assistance and market access, and ensures quality and timely products to the lead firm.
B. Receivables financing	
5. Trade receivables finance	A bank or other financier advances working capital to agribusiness (supplier, processor, marketing and export) companies against accounts receivable or confirmed orders to producers. Receivables financing takes into account the strength of the buyer's purchase and repayment history.
6. Factoring	Factoring is a financial transaction whereby a business sells its accounts receivable or contracts of sales of goods at a discount to a specialized agency, called a factor, who pays the business minus a factor discount and collects the receivables when due. Factoring speeds working capital turnover, credit risk protection, accounts receivable bookkeeping and bill collection services. It is useful for advancing financing for inputs or sales of processed and raw outputs that are sold to reliable buyers.
7. Forfaiting	A specialized forfaitor agency purchases an exporter's receivables of freely-negotiable instruments (such as unconditionally-guaranteed letters of credit and 'to order' bills of exchange) at a discount, improving exporter cash-flow, and takes on all the risks involved with the receivables.
C. Physical asset collateralization	
8. Warehouse receipts	Farmers or other value chain enterprises receive a receipt from a certified warehouse that can be used as collateral to access a loan from third party financial institutions against the security of goods in an independently controlled warehouse. Such systems ensure quality of inventory, and enable sellers to retain outputs and have opportunity to sell for a higher price during the off-season or other later date.

Instrument	Brief description
9. Repurchase agreements (repos)	A buyer receives securities as collateral and agrees to repurchase those at a later date. Commodities are stored with accredited collateral managers who issue receipts with agreed conditions for repurchase. Repurchase agreements provide a buy-back obligation on sales, and are therefore employed by trading firms to obtain access to more and cheaper funding due to that security.
10. Financial lease (lease-purchase)	A purchase on credit which is designed as a lease with an agreement of sale and ownership transfer once full payment is made (usually in instalments with interest). The financier maintains ownership of said goods until full payment is made making it easy to recover goods if payment is not made, while allowing agribusinesses and farmers to use and purchase machinery, vehicles and other large ticket items, without requiring the collateral otherwise needed for such a purchase.

D. Risk mitigation products

11. Insurance	Insurance products are used to reduce risks by pooling regular payments of clients and paying out to those affected by disasters. Payment schedules are set according to statistical data of loss occurrence and mitigate the effects of loss to farmers and others in the value chain from natural disasters and other calamities.
12. Forward contracts	A forward contract is a sales agreement between two parties to buy/sell an asset at a set price and at a specific point of time in the future, both variables agreed to at the time of sale. Forward contracts allow price hedging of risk and can also be used as collateral for obtaining credit.
13. Futures	Futures are forward contracts (see definition above) that are standardized to be traded in futures exchanges. Standardization facilitates ready trading through commodity exchanges. Futures provide price hedging, allowing trade companies to offset price risk of forward purchases with counterbalancing of futures sales.

E. Financial enhancements

14. Securitization instruments	Cash-flow producing financial assets are pooled and repackaged into securities that are sold to investors. This provides financing that might not be available to smaller or shorter-term assets and includes instruments such as collateralized debt obligations, while reducing the cost of financing on medium and longer term assets.
15. Loan guarantees	Agricultural loan guarantees are offered by 3rd parties (private or public) to enhance the attractiveness of finance by reducing lending risks. Guarantees are normally used in conjunction with other financial instruments, and can be offered by private or public sources to support increased lending to the agricultural sector.
16. Joint venture finance	Joint venture finance is a form of shared owner equity finance between private and/or public partners or shareholders. Joint venture finance creates opportunities for shared ownership, returns and risks, partners often have complementary technical, natural, financial and market access resources.

approach can build on and improve these instruments, because of the stronger value chain linkages, and the availability of improved information and communication and other technologies that exist today. The names of the four product financing instruments described are not important but rather they are used to describe a particular way of extending financing. Each of the four has many things in common as well as differences in application, stemming to a large extent from the driver or key actor in the financing.

Trader credit

Trader credit is a traditional form of finance that is prevalent in informal and fragmented agricultural value chains. In these systems, traders, or sometimes trader-farmers, play a critical role in connecting farmers to markets, while providing farmers with funds for harvest, inputs or other needs, such as family emergencies. In many cases traders are members of the rural community who not only have capital and often transportation, but most importantly frequently have specialized knowledge of markets and contacts that enable them to reach those markets. Traders are therefore able to advance funds with the guarantee that the crop to be harvested will be available to them for resale according to the price that is fixed at the time of financing. The funds used by local traders are from a variety of sources – their own equity, financing from banks or wholesalers, and/or they may work as intermediaries of processors or wholesalers who advance them the funds they then use for procuring products from farmers. The trader role in providing financing, especially to small producers is important and well known. Less known is the pressure traders also face both in meeting the need to finance downstream and in dealing with delays of payment that are common from their buyers. As in Box 4.1, they are faced with many demands on their limited available capital which impacts their operational efficiency.

In the many countries without functioning commodity exchanges, prices are often stipulated by the trader on speculation without knowing what the market price or the quality will be at the time of delivery. The prices offered tend to be low to mitigate risk to the trader (who may have advanced credit to tens or hundreds of farmers) and therefore are often disadvantageous to farmers. This trader strategy contributes to the perception that traders are dishonest and cut-throat, and therefore they rarely receive support from development interventions. The many fair trade development initiatives to support small producers are prime examples of alternative trade models that often deliberately eliminate the intermediary role of traders to provide what is considered a better deal to producers.

Traders have long existed because of the critical services they provide to farmers – market linkages, finance and related services (information on

---

Box 4.1 Small-scale farmer capacity and competitiveness, Kenya

Bernard Maina is a trader in Kenya dealing with French beans sourced from smallholders and with a current capacity of 30 tonnes per week. Working with 26 employees, he is able to sell Kshs. 5 million in French beans per month as well as fresh tomatoes worth over Kshs. 2 million monthly. The main challenges facing his enterprise include: upfront payments, equipment and transport, and post harvest losses due to lack of cold room.

Source: Minae and Khisa (2007)

market demand for example) – so understanding the role of traders and trader finance has the potential to provide critical information for sustainable financial and non-financial services, particularly in areas with weak formal farmer organizations. Fries and Akin (2004) have cited the advantages of trader credit in terms of quicker provision of credit, technical assistance and limited collateral requirements, if any. Others have found (Vorley et al., 2008) that market linkages through traders provide a type of quasi-cooperation amongst farmers that can be a building block for a more formal structure.

Traders may in turn receive finance from other value chain businesses such as millers and processors who may themselves be financed from wholesalers or exporters who are farther 'up' the chain from production to marketing. The chains of agreements that include rural traders tend to be informal, while integrated and structured systems generally do not incorporate the trader role. The next case in Box 4.2 of trader finance in Latin America examines how

---

Box 4.2 Trader finance in Latin America

FAO studies of trader working capital confirm the thesis that traders finance their operations from a combination of sources. Major differences were found among countries. As shown below, owner's equity is at the top of the list, making up 40 to 80 per cent of the total. In second and third place is financing received from other agents in the agricultural value chain, ranging from 10 to 30 per cent. This is very similar to institutional financing available to these enterprises, obviously with higher percentages in certain countries, such as Costa Rica. In Ecuador and Peru, a very important source of trader financing comes from moneylenders, in some cases as high as 20 per cent. A similar result was found in Asia.

Sources of working capital	Share of total financing (%)
Owner's equity	40–80
Commercial relations in the agricultural chain	10–30
Institutional financing (important in Costa Rica)	10–30
Moneylenders (important in Ecuador)	10–20
Family and friends	0–1

Before these findings can be used for policy actions, careful consideration must be given to the characteristics of relevant chains and the environment in selected countries. The first important point is the nature of the chain itself, especially the degree of informality. Ecuador and Peru are countries where informal agricultural chains are common, and studies have shown that 25 per cent of the transactions conducted in Peru are informal. The chains in these countries are fragmented. Peru alone has hundreds of thousands of producers, nearly 1,000 mills and 60,000 rice warehouses, standing in contrast to the chains in Argentina and Brazil, which are increasingly concentrated and integrated. These characteristics are very important, because the participants in informal chains tend to be smaller and have less access to financing. Argentina and Brazil also have small-scale producers, but they are members of strong cooperative movements and generally participate in formal systems where the modern retail trade is picking up a fast-growing share of the market.

In conclusion, the study found that trade can survive in the absence of adequate institutional or other financing, but its growth is slowed. Drawing lessons microfinance institutions, certain countries have begun to respond to the demands of agricultural traders. They now offer financing with flexible amounts, lines of credit, alternative forms of collateral, other financial products and above all, offices located near the traders.

Source: Quirós (2007); Gálvez (2006b); Shepherd (2004)

traders are able to finance their operations and their trading with small-scale producers.

Throughout the world, whether for export trade or local trader finance, the most efficient method of financing for the borrower is access to open account lines of credit that can be drawn on when needed. Timing is critical for trade financing. By increasing the availability of financing that can be readily accessed when needed, more funds can flow into the value chain not only benefiting the traders but also those upwards and downwards in the chain who can receive more financing if needed, and potentially higher prices due to less rationing of the trader's cash available.

From an overall value chain finance approach, trader finance is one of a number of ways to provide financing. Its role must be understood from the perspective of those involved as shown in the next section.

Input supplier credit

Like trader credit, input supplier credit is a common form of in-kind financing to farmers at all levels, both in a fragmented and informal agricultural system and in strongly linked value chains in developing and developed countries. Input supplier credit enables farmers to realize a cash flow benefit to access supplies or even equipment for production purposes in a timely fashion. Suppliers provide this because credit is a critical marketing tool to make their inputs and goods more attractive for sale. Yet, the financing results in a drain on the cash flow of their business. Consequently, suppliers often offer cash discounts to improve their cash flow and reduce the risks of non-payment in the future. The key agricultural inputs – seed, fertilizer, agro-chemicals, equipment and fuel – are commonly financed in turn by their suppliers. The supplier in turn may be financed by borrowing secured by the invoices based upon the strength of the sales and repayment records. Nevertheless, collection and account management can be difficult. Consequently, due to their limitations in providing financing and in ensuring repayment, more and more input supplier credit is done indirectly through a triangular relationship in which the input supplier facilitates finance through a financial organization so the buyers can pay the input suppliers. This has the advantage of letting financial entities handle the financing using their expertise and the systems they have in place to do so (Miller, 2007b). It also frees up funds for increasing inventory.

Input supplier credit is relationship based, and suppliers or buyers prefer to extend inputs to local input supply retailers or to farmers whom they have known for a considerable time. For retailers, finance may be given directly in-kind by advancing products on consignment or commission. For proven clients this can work well, but for others it can be problematic. When providing inputs to farmers, it is much riskier since the products may be used in their fields making recovery difficult if crop or other failures occur.

An advantage of the supplier providing finance to the farmer is that it can reduce the farmer's transaction costs, since interest is embedded and paperwork is minimized, and it secures sales. However, this route ties the farmer to one particular supplier and he/she is therefore unable to take advantage of what might be cheaper offers in the market. For input suppliers, providing credit facilitates sales. These suppliers also often know the farmers and reduce their risks by being able to choose to whom to offer credit or not. In addition, they have a vested interest to provide their clients technical advice since they are dependent on the success and trustworthiness of the farmer, all of which helps to strengthen the linkages of the value chain.

Due to a weak private sector, and poorly developed value chains, input suppliers and to a lesser extent traders, agro-processors and agri-businesses, play the most important role in financing to farmers in Myanmar. Historically, input supplier credit and trader credit were often the only two options open to farmers and remain the most important at present. However, as shown in the Myanmar case in Box 4.3, input supplier credit, while being important, can itself be constrained by weaknesses in the value chain.

Access to sufficient and non-expensive financing depends upon the financial services available in the country as well as the strength of the value chain. Even though Myanmar has strong agro-industries in certain sectors, their role in financing down the value chain is constrained by these factors. Similarly, in Africa or Eastern Europe and Central Asia, where fertilizer is a critical input, few fertilizer wholesalers have sufficient conventional collateral that they can pledge against repayment of working capital loans, and banks often do not accept fertilizer as collateral for loans. Without financial links with importers or foreign exporters who can pass input supply credit on to wholesalers, the latter are prevented from operating on a large scale and reducing costs through economies of scale in transport and storage. For fertilizer retailers farther up the value chain, the major challenges involve not only improving access to credit but also developing the capacity to manage input sales on credit without high risks of default on their outstanding accounts.

Box 4.3 Input supply credit, Myanmar

The experiences of the agricultural value chain finance model in Myanmar show that financing is an important issue for the development of agricultural value chains. The private sector providers sell the inputs to farmers on credit, yet this supplier credit rarely stands alone since these companies themselves lack sufficient funding. They need financing which is hard to obtain. In order to recover sales revenue quickly, their preference is cash sales rather than selling inputs to farmers with deferred payment. Consequently, in Myanmar, the agro-input retailers offer deferred payment sales at a high interest cost which results in an inflated price for farmers. The farmers do benefit from at least having access to sales on credit, but it is expensive.

Given that financing is a hindrance for both farmers and their agro-input suppliers, more finance is required in the value chain. More financing is needed farther up the value chain but, currently, the very limited capacity of the banks in rural areas and the fragmented nature of the value chains makes this financing unavailable.

Source: Myint (2007)

Another challenge in some regions of the world is the lack of input suppliers to meet the needs of the producers in their regions. Input suppliers are critical to value chain development. In Africa, for example, the development of agro-dealers is noted as critical for accelerating smallholders' access to quality agricultural inputs and is a focus of development initiatives such as those by the Rockefeller Foundation (World Bank, 2008).

As noted earlier, BRAC has developed a noteworthy approach to input supply and credit by forming supplier businesses and linkages with external suppliers to provide the needed input services, and then advancing loans to farmers to purchase the needed goods.

Unlike BRAC, many input suppliers are small enterprises with limited funds and capacity. Their ability to provide and to receive finance depends to a large extent on the strength of the value chain and its linkages. If strong linkages are present there are opportunities to reduce repayment risk by direct repayment arrangements with the buyers of clients' products and to borrow against the strength of the receivables. In any case, the benefits must be weighed against the disadvantages for each party as shown in Box 4.4.

Box 4.4 Input supplier credit, Bangladesh

BRAC recognized that timely supply of good quality inputs is a major factor that affects enterprise returns and their contribution towards poverty alleviation. Since supply of inputs for different enterprises by the local industries and/or government was not of sufficient quantity/good quality, BRAC established input supply enterprises to supply these inputs, thus improving the incomes and repayment capacities of its agricultural microfinance clients. BRAC's support enterprises in poultry, livestock, agriculture, fisheries and horticulture provide essential inputs to its clients as well as commercial small-scale entrepreneurs in an effort to further strengthen and ensure the maximum return to expand their enterprises. Each of the programmes has three 'wings': 1) extension; 2) production of inputs and processing; and 3) distribution/marketing. This offers a range of package support to different categories of farmers in the agriculture sector in Bangladesh. BRAC provides agriculture support consisting of training, input supply, small and medium enterprise credit and technical assistance.

Source: Saleque in Digal (2009)

Marketing company credit

Buyers from firms such as marketing and processing companies offer finance that works in a similar way to trader credit at the farm level. However, whereas traders tend to run smaller operations and act as intermediaries between farmers and upstream companies, these companies are larger concerns that are acting on their own behalf. Also, this type of credit can be advanced directly to farmers, to farmer organizations and to local traders, as well as being used by larger companies to advance funding to local processors and marketing companies. It is distinguished from lead firm or contract farming finance described in the next section in that this financing is not necessarily part of integrated value chains, but rather is a way of securing purchases and can be a way of providing incentives for loyal customers and traders.

Market company finance or other types of buyer credit are normally driven by the upstream company's product needs for its sales commitments or to fulfil its processing or manufacturing capacity. There often is an established relationship between the company and the producers or producer groups. For these groups it can be beneficial to work with marketing companies since these are closely linked with the market information and have more and often better marketing options. In addition, marketing companies are often able to secure advance sales prices for their commodities and therefore have a more secure basis for setting prices of the products they offer to the traders and producers. Marketing finance is very important worldwide, often the primary source of funding for commodities, even though the relative roles of marketing company finance varies by region and by commodity.

Financing within processors and marketing companies can be upstream as well as downstream. Their financing capacity is often constrained by their own ability to secure financing. Therefore it is common to be 'financed' from some of the clients they buy from who deposit products without receiving full payment until an agreed date, often after the company has had the chance to sell the deposited products or goods processed from them.

The company may or may not directly manage the funding to their clients since they may choose to involve a bank or other financial institution to directly manage disbursements, while collections are managed through receipt of the product. The case of agave in Mexico shown in Box 4.5 provides a straightforward illustration of finance that comes indirectly from a bank through a processing company to farmers.

Box 4.5 Processor finance for agave farmers, Mexico

Agave is a raw material that is grown by smallholder farmers, and is a key ingredient in the production of tequila. Agave production is an interesting example of a value chain, since it is a highly complex activity by comparison with the average farm commodity. It is highly cyclical, grown mainly by small-scale farmers with little access to formal financing, and affected by wild price swings. As such, a banker is unlikely to take on the risk of financing an agave grower. However, the same banker is willing to consider and handle financing for a tequila producer that will use the money to take on the six-year risk of financing a farmer, because he/she understands the value chain and how it works. The banker does not take the risk directly, but provides financing to a company that will take the risk of lending money to the farmer. In other words, the banker will finance a client who needs to guarantee his supply of raw material to keep his own business running. In particular, most tequila producers understand the farming risk because most tequila producers also have their own crops. In a case such as this, the financial institution understands that access to raw materials is a critical factor for the success of the end business. Nevertheless, the bank is not willing to take the risk of financing the primary producer. The flow of financing takes place, in the end, because the farming risk is held by the tequila distiller, who can manage it better than the banks.

Source: Shwedel (2006)

Box 4.6 Marketing company finance, Costa Rica

Chestnut Hill Farms market, and in some cases produce, asparagus, mangoes, melons and pineapples from Arizona, Brazil, California, Costa Rica, Ecuador, Guatemala, Honduras, Peru and Puerto Rico.

Its customers are supermarket chains in the United States. Over the past five years, the company has also been selling to the fresh processed fruit and vegetable sector and supermarket chains in Europe, as well as wholesalers. Its main objective is to add value to production, packaging and marketing. The company handles four trademarks, including 'perfect melon' and 'perfect pineapple'. Consumers are given a 'satisfaction or your money back' guarantee. This helps remove the company from the mass market of generic products or commodities.

The company began with pineapples in Costa Rica in 2002, when exports were running at one or two containers per week; by 2006, it had risen to 70 containers. One reason the company achieved this kind of growth was that it was in the right market at the right time. There was no overproduction, and in general, both production and market risks were low. Another reason is that the company gives financial advances. A budget is drawn up before planting begins, and the money is disbursed gradually as planting progresses. Chestnut Hill Farms also provide agricultural inputs and participate in investments in equipment, infrastructure and materials. Funds are delivered against shipping documents, once products have arrived safely. Each different case requires a separate analysis before partnering and financing. Chestnut Hill Farms is not a financial entity, but it has learned to read signals about where it can and should take risks with the farmers.

Source: Romero (2006)

Buyer credit may also be provided directly by the company as described in the case of Chestnut Hill Farms in Box 4.6. This is possible when the company has ample sources of funds and it wishes to ensure that the production and technology meets its required standards.

Credit from marketing or processor businesses can therefore be as simple as advances from one level of a value chain to another, or integrated into a full chain process as noted in the case of Chestnut Hill Farms agribusiness company. It can also be one of the most important places in the chain where banks and other financiers choose to inject financing due in part to the fact that the repayments can often be directly discounted from proceeds of the products delivered to the marketing company.

Full service types of models for value chain participants are found in various countries. Successful models have been noted in this volume in the cases of BASIX in India, BAAC in Thailand and LAFISE in Latin America. A strong vision, leadership, operational environment and investment have been important toward this success making the model challenging for mass replication.

Lead firm financing

A lead firm is the driver of a value chain, and is typically a large retailer, exporter, processor or distributor that is a recognized market actor. A lead firm commonly takes the initiative to establish a contract or out-grower farming relationship with producers. It can directly provide finance to those under contract. In fact, finance is often a major incentive and binding link between the firm and the producers in such contract farming relationships. Such financing can be in cash advances or more commonly in-kind such as the provision of inputs. However, the lead firm can also directly or indirectly facilitate financing to those in the chain without providing the finance itself. It can set up connections with financing entities or frequently, based on the contractual relationship, producers are able to access finance through a third party. The case of Starbucks in Central America in Box 4.7, illustrates how a retailer can reach down into a value chain and affect financing arrangements through more formal sales contracts.

As noted in the previous chapter, lead firms often operate on the basis of contracts, such as contract farming. Lead firm financing is a 'service package' and is noted as a financial instrument only because of the overarching nature of the financial application. It combines directed credit (i.e. specific use credit), guaranteed markets, fixed price or pricing parameters, technical assistance, and strict standards and delivery commitments. The financing can typically be used only for the sector or for the specific use indicated in the contract, but the source of the financing can be either from the lead firm itself or by arrangement or facilitation with a third party such as Root Capital, noted in Box 4.7, or from a bank or other financial entity.

Box 4.7 Lead firm finance and assistance in Central America

The Starbucks Coffee Company has more than 10,000 coffee shops around the world. Starbucks consciously seeks out a wide diversity of suppliers, currently buying coffee in more than 127 countries. It seeks a direct relationship with its growers who can systematically provide it with high quality products. The company has developed a detailed set of socially responsible standards and operates supplier certification programmes both for agricultural products (C.A.F.E. practices) and for non-agricultural products (such as glasses and napkins used in the restaurants). For small coffee producers, it finds that many follow good practices and one of Starbuck's main tasks it to help them become more organized and orderly in their processes.

Coffee companies, like Starbucks, have found that pre-finance is important for the coffee-growers' associations to be able to pre-finance the farmers' harvest and the local processing and preparation for export. It does not see its role as their banker; rather when producers are organized and with a good product and reliable market, financing from financial institutions and/or specialized financial funds is made possible. Starbucks does not want to provide direct financing and decided to invest through socially oriented commercial financing companies or organizations such as Root Capital (previously named EcoLogic Finance) and the Calvert Foundation investment fund. Root Capital, for example, provides pre-financing to coffee cooperatives, along with technical advice and uses the Starbucks sales contracts as collateral. Although not necessarily cheaper than bank loans, this credit is much more flexible. Farmers need only show their sales contract with Starbucks to be considered creditworthy. It is typically very short-term credit until harvest, but in some cases, farmers have also been able to use credit to invest in infrastructure and processing equipment. When the products are shipped, Starbucks pays the company directly for interest and principal payments. Because of this model, Root Capital has been able to maintain a repayment rate of over 99 per cent.

Source: Torrebiarte (2006)

Product financing instruments are very important, especially in the lower end of the value chain. Yet, because of linkages these instruments can also be useful to banks and other financial institutions that provide financing to the chain, since they allow financing to agribusinesses higher in the chain that can then provide financing through the chain to those further down. For example, financing the farmers indirectly through the agribusiness may be less costly and risky. Key benefits and limitations for key groups of agricultural value chain actors are highlighted in Table 4.2.

Table 4.2 Benefits and limitations of product financing

Benefits	Limitations
1. Producers	
• Market information and advice (e.g. what to grow).	• Monopolistic business and farmers do not wish to risk the relationship by seeking other buyers.
• Access to inputs on an as-need basis.	
• Avail market linkage (both forwards and backwards) at an agreed terms reduces price risk.	• Pricing is often disadvantageous to farmers.
• Often lower-cost transportation of inputs and produce.	• Market information may be withheld (e.g. buyers, pricing).
• Technical assistance.	• Cost is often high (higher prices on credit and high direct or embedded interest rates).
• Loans and advances are relationship based; collateral is not required.	
• Quick and hassle-free funding.	• Quality may not be reliable.
• May get credit for non-agricultural needs, such as family emergencies.	• May stifle innovation and market niche development.
• Low cost of transactions due to multiple services of technical support, markets and finance.	• Funding is usually limited to working capital for a specific sector.
	• Flexibility is limited and comparative pricing is difficult.
2. Agribusiness	
• Assured and increased volume of sales of inputs and avail volume discounts.	• Farmers may side-sell (this is less common in traditional systems with tight family and community relationships).
• Encourages and supports production of desired quality/standard and varieties.	• There are many risks related to production, markets and prices.
• Assured supply of produce and onward movement up in the value chains (e.g. processors).	• Farmers may not pay or may delay payment.
• Guaranteed supply can stimulate finance to firms receiving raw materials (e.g. forward contracting).	• Smaller agribusinesses are often not equipped to manage accounts receivables finance.
• Vulnerability of farmers from a lack of funds may enable them to take advantage and offer low prices.	• Accounts receivable outstanding may limit inventory purchases and sales.
	• Not all services are profitable and multiple, diverse activities can be difficult to manage.
3. Financial intermediaries	
• Economies of scale can be achieved by lending through the agribusiness entities.	• Economies of scale only achievable in case of higher volume of finance at a lower rate.
• Point of Sales (PoS) financing is possible which can reduce the cost of transactions.	• IT system may not support Point-of-Sales (PoS) transactions.

Receivables financing

Receivables backed financing (often for export) is a general term for financing which is secured by accounts receivables and sales contracts. In this type of financial product, normally a loan is made in cash or in-kind whereby security is provided by the assignment of those receivables and the repayment comes from the sales proceeds directly to the lender. Inventory financing, which is described later, is similar in the sense that the future sale of a good or commodity will provide the borrower with the means to repay the financing.

Receivables finance includes bills discounting, invoice discounting and payment protection. This finance is often tailored to meet the individual requirements of the suppliers and buyer involved, enabling them to accelerate cash flow from sales and mitigate risks. The ultimate goal of integrated trade based financial instruments is to mediate the way the various clients acquire, move, monitor and pay for goods within value chains. Successful deployment of financial supply chain solutions requires close coordination with multiple stakeholders dealing with procurement, logistics, finance, account management, and various types of risk.

Trade receivables finance

Many names and terms are used to describe receivable financing. In regards to agricultural value chains, the term is most commonly used in relation to trade finance and therefore is the focus of the following section. It is used most often in import–export finance as opposed to trade within a country or region. The term, trade receivables finance, is defined broadly in this section to include: pre-finance, supplier finance, purchase order finance and export finance. It could also include factoring and forfaiting which are treated in the following section in order to clarify their specific nature and use.

Receivables finance is a method used by businesses to convert sales on credit terms for immediate cash flow. Financing accounts receivable is a financial tool for obtaining flexible working capital in which the receivable credit line is determined by the financial strength of the customer (buyer), not the client (seller of the receivables). Receivables may be of cross border or domestic origin. Where there is a weak credit environment, such that collection is difficult, receivables financing has been primarily for export receivables, especially where the buyer is from a country with a stronger financial environment whereby default arbitration is easier. This characteristic of export receivables allows exporters to use it as an alternative source of financing when conventional financing is difficult due to the lack of a supportive financing environment in its own country.

Export and import financing fit within a broader category of trade finance which is typically used for international trade. With increased use of the Internet for information on emerging markets, suppliers are now directly engaging with their buyers in other countries. A dynamic shift is taking place in transaction processes which increase efficiency for the benefit of both importers and exporters. It is important to note that international receivables financing is often directly applicable only for major companies in the value chain but its influence can be felt by participants throughout the value chain.

In the illustration in Figure 4.1, the lending bank advances funds to a producer to provide working (and sometimes investment) finance. In return, the bank is given an assignment of future receivables from the buyer of the goods. Importantly, this assignment is acknowledged by the buyer, who will make payments in line with the schedule in the commercial contact with the producer. These payments will go to a collection account in the bank, from which they are transferred to a debt reserve account. At the loan repayment dates, money is taken from the debt service account, in-line with the repayment obligations of the borrower. While an agreed level of reserve must be maintained in the debt service account, any other money accruing from buyers' payments is remitted back to the producer.

One of the most critical periods for financing farmers is at harvest then their financial reserves from the last harvest often fall short and they commonly turn to money lenders or local traders for funding at often exorbitant interest rates and/or pre-harvest sales at low prices. Many farmers have indicated that pre-financing is often more important than the price, since the money is so desperately needed for living or hiring labour for harvest. However, with strong value chain linkages, pre-financing advances can be secured by receivables of product from the upcoming harvest. This concept of trade finance also holds true for advancing funds against products or receivable obligations elsewhere in the value chain. In summary, trade finance, which provides funding structured around purchases and sales transactions, guaranteed by products and accounts receivables, is very important and

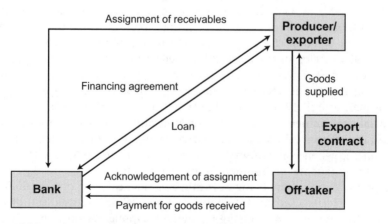

Figure 4.1 Pre-export receivables finance basic scheme
Source: Winn et al. (2009)

widely used. In times of financial crisis it plays an even more important role when other funding is restricted and the overall fear of risk is heightened.

Factoring and forfaiting

Factoring is a financial transaction, in which a business sells its accounts receivable (i.e. invoices) at a discount. Factoring differs from bank loans in three main ways. First, the emphasis is on the value of the receivables, not the firm's creditworthiness. Secondly, factoring is not a loan – it is the purchase of an asset (the receivables). Finally, a traditional bank loan involves two parties, whereas factoring involves three. As diagrammed in Figure 4.2 the three parties directly involved in a factoring transaction are: the *seller*, the *debtor*, and the *factor* (the specialized financial company). The *seller* (e.g. input supplier or wholesaler) is owed money (usually for products or goods sold) by the buyer of goods, the *debtor*. The *seller* sells its receivable invoices at a discount to the third party, the *factor*, to obtain an advance payment (e.g. 75–85 per cent). Upon notification, the debtor can only legally liquidate the debt by paying to the factor. The debtor then directly pays the factor the full value of the invoice. When the final payment is made from the debtor, the factor then pays the seller a final settlement payment (total sale value minus advance, fees and interest.) Most factoring is done on a 'recourse' basis, meaning that if the debtor does not pay despite the efforts of the factor, the factor will have recourse to claim payment from the seller.

Factoring can make funds available even when banks would not do so using conventional lending methods. Since factoring companies are frequently part of banks, either as subsidiaries or divisions of banks, it allows the banks an alternative for financing businesses with insufficient acceptable collateral. The

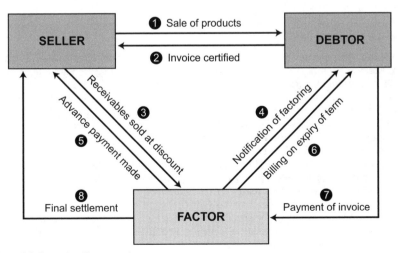

Figure 4.2 Factoring finance scheme
Source: author, Miller

discount factor (cost) varies with the creditworthiness of the debtor, which is often a well known and solvent company, rather than the seller. An agribusiness factors its invoices when it calculates that it will be better off using the proceeds to bolster its own growth than it would be by effectively functioning as its 'customer's bank' – the return on the proceeds will exceed the discount fees and interest costs on the receivables.

In addition to financing, the factor performs two other important services – the collection service of the accounts receivable and the assessment of the credit worthiness of the buyer. The factoring company can be better placed for collection and it may have a better understanding of the condition of a seller's customer than the seller does itself and can warn if the buyer's financial situation, and/or the respective value chain, is deteriorating and advise the seller accordingly. An additional advantage of a factoring company compared to a bank financing is that the former can purchase receivables quickly, efficiently and with great flexibility, so as to meet customers' requirements as shown in Box 4.8.

Reverse Factoring. This offers one solution to barriers to factoring. In the case of reverse factoring, the lender purchases accounts receivables only from specific transparent, high-quality buyers which have sufficient and trust-worthy information to be able to adequately assess. The factor needs to collect credit information and calculate the credit risk for selected buyers, which are often large, internationally accredited firms. Like traditional factoring, which allows a supplier to transfer the credit risk default from itself to its customers, the main advantage of reverse factoring is that the credit risk is equal to the default risk of the selected, high-quality customers, and not the riskier,

---

Box 4.8 Factoring in Serbia

In Serbia, the payments to farmers for the sale of their produce are often delayed. Factoring works well for those needing fast payment. The process is straightforward. The farmer bills its buyers in the usual way except that farmers will be asked to stamp each invoice with a 'notice of assignment' indicating that the invoice has been assigned to a factoring company. This means that the farmer's produce buyer now owes the factoring company the face value of the assigned invoice. The factoring company then advances the farmer's business approximately 75 per cent to 85 per cent of the face value of the invoices. The reserve amount of 15 to 25 per cent that is held back is based on the quality of the accounts rather than on the strength of the farm's business, i.e. the fee fluctuates according to the creditworthiness and performance of the farmer's receivables. The farmer's final payment of the reserve minus the factor fee is received after the buyer pays the factor. The factor fee can be as low as 2 per cent of the invoice amount depending on the level of risk involved. In summary, the benefits of factoring for the farmer are to: 1) improve the cash flow; 2) allow for better financial planning; and 3) allow the farmer to focus on the business and sales rather than collections.

Source: Winn et al. (2009)

lesser known small or medium agribusiness firms. This arrangement allows creditors in developing countries to factor 'without recourse' and provides low-risk financing to higher-risk suppliers.

In Mexico, the Nacional Financiera, S.N.C (Nafinsa) development bank does reverse factoring on a non-recourse basis using an Internet-based platform. This enables any commercial bank to participate and compete to factor suppliers' receivables. The success of the Nafinsa programme depends in part on the legal and regulatory support offered in Electronic Signature and Security laws (Klapper, 2005).

Overall, the use of factoring in agriculture is increasing but widespread use is infrequent in developing countries. However, there is much room for growth for factoring with value chains due to its combined services of finance, collection, debtor assessment and often expediency of services.

Forfaiting. This is a less well known source of financing and collection services which has many similarities to factoring 'without recourse', meaning the forfaiting company assumes all collection risk. It is used for larger, medium-term receivables and is different from the factoring operation in the sense that forfaiting is based on one or more transactions, while factoring is based upon selling all or a quantity of its short-term receivables. For example, in forfaiting, the company purchases an exporter's receivables (the amount the importers owe the exporter) at a discount by paying cash. The forfaitor, who is the purchaser of the receivables, becomes the entity to whom the importer is obliged to pay its dept. By purchasing these receivables, which are usually guaranteed by the importer's bank, the forfaitor frees the exporter from the risk of not receiving payment from the importer's purchases on credit, while giving the exporter a cash payment. It therefore allows the importer to essentially buy on credit. When well established, the receivables can be traded as bills of exchange or promissory notes, which are debt instruments.

Summary assessment of receivables financing. The use of receivables financing is growing in line with the growth of value chain integration and global markets. The various instruments are heavily used in international trade finance and to a lesser extent in domestic finance within value chains. Due to its direct relationship with trade and its short-term nature, it is impacted by financial crisis, such as occurred in 2008 and 2009. Yet, it also showed greater resilience in repayments compared with other lending products (Subjally, 2009). As shown in Table 4.3, it has significant potential as well as limitations which affect its use.

Table 4.3 Benefits and disadvantages of receivables financing

Benefits	Disadvantages
Farmers	
Suppliers and buyers have more financing that can be passed to them.	
Agribusiness companies	
Easier access to financing based on strength of clients and purchase/sale.	Pricing may be higher.
Negotiable to fit the specific nature of the value chain.	Lead firms can be monopolistic.
Can reduce transaction costs of trade finance, such as allowing more use of open trade accounts which are less costly than secured ones.	Requires policies and regulations that are often lacking or inadequate in developing countries.
Can improve account receivable collection efficiency and risk.	Risks related to production, markets and prices still exist.
Widely used by medium and large businesses involved in trade.	Not viable for many micro and small agribusinesses.
Financial institutions	
Strong business line opportunity for the bank and clients.	Requires awareness and specialized services and skills, such as with factoring and forfaiting.
Reduces collateral requirements needed for loans while providing security.	Risks related to production, markets and prices.

Physical asset collateralization

A key concept of value chain financing is to use the chain and its products and transactions for securing finance. In agriculture this involves some physical commodity or asset. Financing secured by commodities or moveable assets can often be achieved even when the value chain linkages are weak or fragmented. Of course, modern, more secure value chains which have strong linkages, secured markets and/or storage, commonly accepted grades and standards, and operate under defined contracts or well established working agreements make physical asset collateralization easier and even more accepted by banking and regulatory organizations. This in turn provides opportunity for obtaining additional financing, less costly financing and/or more flexible financing by reducing or replacing the need for mortgage and other conventional sources of collateral.

Warehouse receipts

Warehouse receipts are an important instrument in value chain financing and much emphasis is devoted to illustrating its use as an instrument of value chain finance. It is a part of the broader term of *inventory finance* whereby the inventory of a commodity or asset serves as the guarantee. In some cases, the credit that is advanced is relationship based and requires no paperwork. More commonly though, inventory credit is a form of collateralization finance known as warehouse receipts. A warehouse receipt system provides both secure storage and access to credit for the value chain actor that 'owns' the inventory – usually a commodity. For example, a producer, trader or processor can store grain in a certified public or private warehouse, receive a receipt for the deposit, and use the stored commodity as collateral against a loan from a lending institution. Because these commodities are stored in a licensed warehouse, the receipt proves both that the commodities are physically in the warehouse and that they are safe and secured. This receipt serves as the guarantee or collateral basis for financing, whereas in traditional lending, the underlying collateral is only a secondary source of repayment that needs to be mobilized when something goes wrong. In collateralized commodity lending, it is the first source of repayment.

Approaches and applications of warehouse receipts. Warehouse receipts are used extensively around the globe with examples presented here from Latin America, Asia and Africa. A typical warehouse receipt system involves a managed warehouse that issues receipts for stored commodities, the owner of the stored commodity acquires the receipt to use as collateral, and a financial institution accepts the receipt as collateral and provides loans against the receipt. Figure 4.3 from HDFC Bank, India, illustrates the connections between the various aspects of a warehouse receipt system.

In this case, HDFC Bank works with a trusted collateral management company in a three-way partnership with the farmer borrower. The management

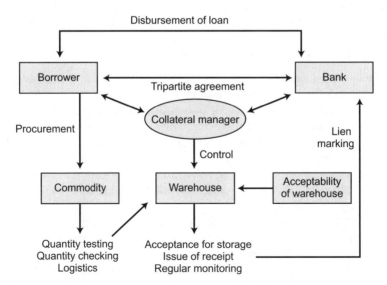

Figure 4.3 HDFC Bank warehouse system
Source: Ananthakrishnan (2007)

company holds responsibility of the warehouse management, quality control and the issuance of receipts allowing the bank to concentrate on its direct banking functions with the borrower. With the security of the warehouse receipts and ease of redemption in case of default, it can then provide financing to more clients often at lower rates.

Formal warehouse receipt system. A formal warehouse receipt system is frequently highly structured and regulated to ensure its security – not only product security and quality but also that the receipt is a recognized legal document that can be used by banks and courts. Warehouse receipts are negotiable and can be redeemed for inventory of the same grade and value as that for which a receipt was originally written. As such, warehouse receipts facilitate the conversion of illiquid farm product inventories into cash, and improve the tradability and liquidity of underlying commodity markets. Warehouse receipt systems allow farmers or traders to create 'bankable' collateral through the deposit of non-perishable commodities in warehouses, while third-party asset (warehouse) managers control and safeguard the quantity and quality of the product in the interest of holders of the negotiable warehouse receipts. While simple in concept, a well functioning warehouse receipt system requires that commodity grades and standards be generally accepted within the trading community and often require regulatory policies which are not present in many developing countries.

There are many variations on the basic warehouse receipt model as well as differences in the execution and enabling environments that are described below. Box 4.9 illustrates a formal warehouse receipt system that results in finance to both fisherman and farmers and the buyers/processors of their produce. In this case in the Philippines, working capital is made available through the use of the CAR warehouse receipts. The loans are self liquidating to the bank through discounting the loans at the time of sale of processed goods to buyers, thus reducing cost and risk to the lender.

Informal warehouse receipt system. A well managed system does not need to be so formal to offer more limited warehouse financing functions. Such alternatives may offer opportunities for poorer and more remote farmers to participate in warehouse receipt financing when more formal structures are not possible. For example, FAO has found that relatively simple community level systems for warehouse receipts can work well where there is sufficient local or regional organizations and community interest to ensure transparency and quality (Miller, 2007b). Regardless of informal or formal, some organizational structures must be in place.

Figure 4.4 illustrates how Development International Desjardins (DID) has adapted the warehouse receipt approach to work with farmers and SACCOs (Savings and Credit Cooperative Organizations) in different parts of Africa. In Madagascar, for example, 850 farmers participate in Desjardin's warehouse receipt project with loans totalling approximately US$1 million, with a repayment rate of 98 per cent (Boily and Julien, 2007). Figure 4.4 depicts the process

Box 4.9 Formal agri-fishery warehouse receipts, Philippines

The Quedan and Rural Credit Guarantee Corporation (QUEDANCOR) is a government corporation attached to the Department of Agriculture, established in 1978 to support the production and marketing of the country's major staples – rice and corn. Over the years, QUEDANCOR financing became available for fruits, vegetables, meat, poultry, sugar and aqua culture products. The QUEDANCOR Financing Program for Working Capital of Buyers and Processors of Agri-Fishery Commodities (QFPWCL) was designed to help fish farmers obtain immediate cash, and at the same time provide additional working capital for the buyers and/or processors of the farmers' produce. In effect, it provides credit assistance to the key players in the agricultural value chain. Specifically, it adopts an inventory financing scheme wherein the buyers/processors of agri-fishery commodities can avail of loan based on Commodity Acknowledgement Receipts (CAR). The CAR is a document issued by the buyer/processor to fish farmers for commodities delivered for processing.

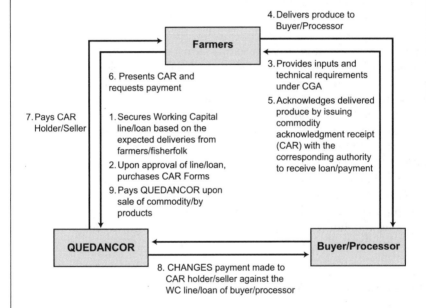

First, the buyer/processor of the agri-fishery commodities applies for a working capital loan with QUEDANCOR based on their expected delivery from farmers with whom they have an existing contract or agreement. Upon approval of the working capital loan, the buyer/processor purchases CAR forms from QUEDANCOR in accordance with the expected deliveries. After the delivery of produce by the farmers, the buyer/processor issues CARs as proof of the delivered commodity, as well as a corresponding 'authority to receive' working capital loan authorization. The CARs can then be submitted to QUEDANCOR by the farmer for actual payment for the delivery of produce. The buyer/processor, on the other hand, forwards to QUEDANCOR their loan payment after the sale of processed goods to institutional buyers. Overall, the QPWCL programme maximizes the potential of the stakeholders within the value chain by ensuring that each function is interdependent to each individual player. Hence, growth is encouraged as smooth value chain functioning leads to a successful outcome.

Source: Digal (2009)

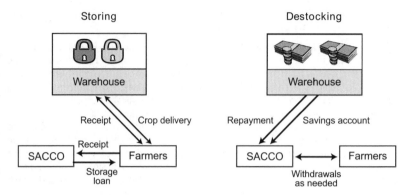

Figure 4.4 SACCO Cooperative warehouse storage
Source: Boily and Julien (2007)

for the delivery and storage of a crop by a farmer to a warehouse. Upon delivery of the crop for storage, the farmer receives a receipt. This is taken to the SACCO where a storage loan is given, thus enabling the farmer to receive cash and yet be able to sell the crop at a later, and usually more advantageous, date.

In the 'destocking' process the stored produce is sold from the warehouse and payment is made directly to the SACCO to repay the loan. The surplus funds from the sale are deposited into the farmer's savings account in the SACCO. The farmer is then free to withdraw funds as needed.

Desjardins has also applied this approach in Tanzania where the role of SACCOs has continually been recognized as a farmer-owned system that can be equipped and evolved to avail a wider range of products to its members including warehouse receipts. This more informal context for a warehouse receipt system based on SACCOs is detailed in Box 4.10.

Box 4.10 Informal warehouse receipts, Tanzania

Desjardin has found that the SACCO's (Savings and Loan Cooperative) proximity to small-scale farmers in Tanzania can offer better access to financial services and contribute to improved value chain finance performance and increased incomes of rural families. The contribution of SACCOs to the functioning of value chains has ranged from: increased productivity though access to capital for inputs and equipment; adding value to agricultural products through loans for processing and packaging; bringing products to consumers through loans to distributors or retailers; and enhancing provision of food security in the community through financing storage.

The proximity and the scope offered by savings and credit cooperatives are powerful levers that can considerably facilitate, at all steps of a value chain, the transfer of money that supports the flow of produce from the field to the end consumer's food basket. Desjardins has learned in Tanzania that this lever is much more powerful and effective when lasting partnerships can be established between the different players who support an agricultural system – for example, agreements between buyers and producers for the sale of crops that instil confidence in the lending organization.

Source: Boily and Julien (2007)

The examples in Box 4.10 work because of the level of organization, trust and close linkages between the farmers, warehouses and SACCOs, as well as start-up capacity building by DID. Together these compensate for the lack of a formal warehouse receipt programme. Even so, an inadequate regulatory environment was noted as a constraint and would likely become more important for expansion with non-SACCO members and to commodities with greater complexity of grading and storing.

Field warehousing. A variation on a centralized warehouse receipt system is 'field warehousing' where inventory is maintained close to production sites, even though the warehouse headquarters are centrally located. This reduces transport costs and improves accessibility to warehousing at time of harvest. However, processes for sound administration, regular inspection and quality control are critical elements of a field warehousing system. Building on the Tanzania case, the following case in Box 4.11 outlines the National Bulk Handling Corporation's (NBHC) management approach to distributed storage facilities.

Public vs. private warehouses. Warehouses that issue receipts can be either publicly or privately owned. While there has been much growth in private warehousing, governments have traditionally played an important role in this activity in some countries. Some form part of government strategies for food reserves or to stabilize prices. In either case, the receipts that are issued by a storage facility need to be recognized by lending institutions as worthwhile collateral. This means that the management processes described above must be in place. Typically, even when warehouses are privately owned and operated, the government provides standardized and recognized inspection and certification services. However, as stated by Ramana (2007a), there is an immense need for quality warehousing facilities and a need for their acceptability and use by the overall commodity market financing system. An example of how this operates on a public level is noted in the case of the Philippines in Box 4.12.

Box 4.11 Field warehousing, India

The National Bulk Handling Corporation (NBHC) has found that farmers in India realize only about 30–35 per cent value of the value of their produce compared to 65–70 per cent in developed economies. It considers that the agri-produce marketing system in India is inefficient and fragmented and that warehouses, their management, and receipts issued by them do not enjoy market confidence which hinders the development of the industry. Recent initiatives by NBHC to overcome this issue include collateral management agreements with eight leading banks; warehouse receipts that incorporate security features to reduce the risk of forgery; extensive use of information technology in all operations; mobile commodity testing; and in-house commodity protection services. As part of this programme, NBHC field warehousing maintains custody of inventory at specific monitored locations that are connected to the administrative control system, that in turn links to the banks. In order to guarantee the condition and security of stored goods at field warehouses, NBHC obtains regular audit and stock condition intelligence through an in-house team, conducts quality testing, administers security, and manages the health of the stored goods.

Source: Choudhary (2007)

Box 4.12 Publicly controlled warehouses, Philippines

The government of the Philippines operates the National Food Authority's (NFA) Corn Storage Programme and Palay Negotiable Warehouse Receipt system. The former issues NFA master passbooks to individual corn farmers who have corn stock at NFA, along with free storage. The passbook can be used as loan collateral with specific financing institutions. Similarly, in the latter programme, warehouse receipts are issued to palay rice farmer organizations and may also be used as collateral for commodity loans from the same financial institutions.

Source: Mangabat (2007)

Warehouse receipts in the wider context. Warehouse receipt systems also need to be understood within the larger context. Their application and strength goes beyond merely being a source of collateral for financing. Very often they are often combined with other finance instruments and non-financial services that conjointly enable a comprehensive set of value chain services. The example from India in Box 4.13 describes a 'one-stop shop' that overcomes barriers in development of the agricultural sector by drawing on a range of interlinked financial and commodity management activities.

The Indian example of combining logistics, warehousing, financing and marketing is important for improving efficiency in the value chain. Even so, its use is largely limited to those commodities with non-perishable products with relatively predictable price rises. Otherwise warehousing is generally not warranted. However, new models have been developed to apply warehouse receipts beyond easily stored commodities such as grain. In Mexico, the use of warehouse receipts has been expanded from non-perishables to include

---

Box 4.13 Agricultural warehouse receipts in the wider system, India

In order to address the current stagnation in the agriculture sector, and to address specific farmer problems, a new agro trade, finance and risk management 'ecosystem' is being undertaken jointly by the Multi-Commodity Exchange (MCX India), the National Spot Exchange Ltd (NSEL), and the National Bulk Handling Corporation (NBHC), a warehouse management company, in India. Under the ecosystem, the commodity exchanges provide a trading platform that facilitates access to credit for farmers and other value chain participants. Commodity exchanges also provide daily prices and signal changes in commodity movements, and assist financial institutions and agribusinesses in commodity portfolio management. In addition, commodity futures and spot exchanges provide points of reference support to make crop and marketing decisions and up to a certain extent balance the demand and supply.

NBHC provides access to warehouse and financing services through a nationwide network of storage and bulk handling facilities. It ensures access to and assurance of year-round business from a nation-wide network of clients. In addition to offering secure collateral management, NBHC provides its clients easy and low-cost finance through bank agreements, thus reducing dependency on seasonal price variations, and saving farmers from distressed, pre-harvest sales. It increases cost-effective financial and operational efficiencies to clients by providing single-window, hassle-free, customized end-to-end solutions. The system increases the bargaining capacity of farmers and provides a platform where they can sell the produce to any buyer across the country. In addition, through the NSEL spot exchange, it allows farmers to quote their own price. Such facilitation can lead to reduced intermediation costs and higher prices and returns.

Source: Rutten et al. (2007)

shrimp and livestock. Whereas grains can be stored and sold when pricing is favourable, livestock and especially seafood have a shorter window of opportunity. Accordingly, the importance of understanding the market is highlighted as even more important (Martinez, 2006).

Reducing warehouse receipt risk through commodity management. In order to reduce risk in a warehouse receipt system – both for the producer and the credit institution – it is critical to ensure that standards and regulations are understood and observed, warehouses are well managed, receipts are recognized collateral, and that transparency exists throughout the system. Specialized commodity management companies are relatively new but are beginning to play an important role in facilitating value chain financing through the services they provide in commodity management, risk control and financial facilitation. With increasingly integrated value chain systems, risks anywhere in the chain have significant consequences. These risks go well beyond the warehouse and include the spectrum of logistics management of transport, handling, financing, contracting and communications. Commodity managers who specialize in these services can help to make warehouse receipt programmes and value chain financing more efficient and often more viable because of their services.

ACE is a global leader in agricultural and other commodities. Their primary service is that of guaranteeing continuous monitoring and control of trading assets, such as commodities, which are used by businesses as collateral to secure a working capital. Box 4.14 summarizes ACE's approach to risk mitigation. Commodity management services are simple in principle – they provide assurance of quantity, quality and timeliness of products and contractual commitments as well as assisting in arranging and facilitating finance. Warehouse management is central, but often only one part of their larger workload.

Benefits and challenges of inventory finance and warehouse receipts. The application of inventory finance and warehouse receipts is 'positive-sum'. This means that available working (collateralizable) assets remain inside the chain, while additional funds flow in from the outside, thanks to the existence of contracts assuring commitment to the products. Contracts become an intangible security which replaces traditional forms of collateral (Gonzalez-Vega in Quirós, 2007: 52). Secure inventory contracts ensure the ability to repay which can allow banks, SACCOs and other financiers to offer lower interest rates than otherwise would be possible.

The most common forms of collateral-based financing use real estate as collateral to secure a loan. Under such credit programmes, credit recipients mortgage their fixed assets such as plantations, plants or storage facilities. These assets are limited and often insufficient. Furthermore, they do not measure the repayment capacity of the business. As described above, collateral may also take the form of commodities and goods as well as livestock, forest products, manufactured goods or input supplies deposited in a warehouse, thus expanding the options for financing. Furthermore, negotiable and transferable warehouse receipts can have a positive impact on agricultural markets and price.

Box 4.14 ACE and global risk mitigation

Warehouse receipting developed into a highly dynamic field that integrates financial services into agricultural value chains based on negotiable or non-negotiable terms. In order to keep risk to a minimum, ACE believes it is necessary to develop systems that are based on a stable legal framework aimed at comprehensively protecting all the players in the market.

ACE has been practicing warehouse receipting for 11 years in 73 countries and highlights key parameters for success as follows:

- reliability as a key requirement for all players;
- quality and weight controls subjected to all transactions;
- monitoring and control services;
- processes must integrate production, distribution and collection;
- insurance, well established along the value chain;
- financing and structuring opportunities.

Credit risk mitigation is achieved by focusing on the commodity rather than the client. The transaction processes are guided by various models which include components such as:

- contracts;
- identification and verification;
- pricing;
- controls;
- other risk mitigation methods.

Source: Soumah (2007)

Despite the perceived and often realized benefits of warehouse receipt financing, it has remained illusive in many parts of the world. Firstly, warehouses are often not available or secure and regulation is not in place to allow banks to use receipts as collateral for financing, etc. Secondly, even for commodities which can be easily graded and stored price cycles may not be predictable, governmental price interventions or imports may increase risk of storage, and other such marketing factors may also impede its use. Finally, awareness, trust and confidence in warehouse management and fulfilment of contracts may be lacking. A summary of the benefits and challenges is presented in Table 4.4.

Although a warehouse receipt system is advantageous to the financing of a value chain, there are challenges and risks to be addressed in order to set up and implement the system. This often requires support and collaboration by development agencies and the private sector to build both the capacity and to put in place the regulations and infrastructure required. An example of such collaboration is shown in Kenya and Tanzania:

In Kenya, IFAD and ACE worked with the government to help develop the Warehouse Receipt Act of 2005 and IFAD and the Government of Tanzania signed a Loan Agreement in 2002 to finance the Agricultural Marketing System Development Programme for agricultural marketing policy development (warehouse receipt act, taxation and marketing policy). (Cherogony, 2007)

Table 4.4 Benefits and challenges of inventory finance and warehouse receipts

Benefits and advantages	Challenges and disadvantages
Security:	*Security:*
• Default rates on payment of non-real estate collateralized loans tend to be low. • The borrower (producer) repays the loan with earnings on sale of the product. • If the borrower or depositor of the merchandise under warrant does not pay, the creditor can call on the warrant company to execute the goods given as security, normally by means of public auction. • If anything happens to the goods on deposit, the warehouse assumes responsibility. • In the case of disputes between creditors, the law generally grants precedence to a title of ownership.	• Formal systems require clearly defined regulation. • Warehouse management needs to be competent as well as transparent. • Regulated warehouses are not always accessible, particularly to more remote farmers. • Collateral management may be weak or untrustworthy. • Costs of warehousing, security and use of receipts may make warehouse receipts unattractive for some situations. • Informal systems, and even some formal ones, are not fraud proof.
Financing:	*Financing:*
• Financing and liquidity is increased in the value chain due to the collateralization of inventory. • Warehouse receipts can be negotiated and traded. • Potential for lower cost financing due to reduced risk and often direct loan repayment at point of sale. • Potential for reduced transaction costs of borrowing.	• Banks and other lending institutions may not perceive the stored commodity as viable collateral. • The flexibility of the warehouse receipt as a financial instrument varies across contexts. • Strong linkages between warehouse and financial institutions, and between warehouse and markets, are required to enable the system to function properly.
Product and pricing:	*Product and pricing:*
• Potential for higher returns from delayed, off-season selling and increased ability to sell at market price peaks. • Potential for price stabilization in marketplace. • Incentives for improved grades and standards. • Potential for improved food security and reduced product storage losses. • Promotes income evening and seasonal saving.	• Poor infrastructure negatively impacts warehouse receipt systems. • Standards for product quality must be established. • Product price norms may not be predictable and may decrease during storage time. • Many products are perishable or difficult to transport and store efficiently. • Requires capacity building for smallholders to accept warehousing and to realize full potential.

In India, the Central Warehousing Corporation (CWC), with considerable experience in the field, offers its recommendations for dealing with some of the challenges for expanding the use of warehouse receipts (see Box 4.15).

Box 4.15 Warehouse receipt challenges and solutions, India

The Central Warehousing Corporation (CWC) sees potential for making warehouse receipts a widely accepted instrument for facilitating credit against warehoused stocks. However, there are obstacles in the popularization of warehouse-based financing in India. Current limitations include:

- Warehouse receipts lack negotiability as an instrument.
- Insufficiently trained staff at warehouses restrict extension activities.
- Inadequate infrastructure is available for storage, weighing, packaging, handling and transportation of goods.

To overcome these obstacles, CWC recommends there is a need for:

- Regulation of warehousing activities by a central agency.
- Provision of legal status to warehouse receipts as a negotiable instrument.
- Reduction of processes involved in use of warehousing receipts.
- Private sector investments in warehousing.
- Uniform policies for quality control and grade specification.
- Coordination with financing institutions for facilitating singly window clearance.
- Increased use of information technology.

Source: Thomas (2007)

Repurchase agreements (repos)

A repurchase agreement, often referred to as a 'repo', is an agreement between two parties whereby one party sells the other a product or security at a specified price with a commitment to buy it back at a later date for another specified price. Sales made with repurchase buy-back obligations are used to secure the 'loan' by owning the asset. It lowers financial risk and is therefore attractive for trading firms to obtain access to cheaper funding due to the lower risk of loan recovery.

The commodities used in repurchase agreements are typically stored with accredited collateral managers responsible for quality, grading and issuing receipts, which are often transferred to an exchange broker. They work best when a futures market is in place, but only require a functioning spot market such that the commodities can be sold when needed. One repurchase agreement programme in Mexico that deserves mention is used with a warehousing programme as shown in Box 4.16.

Box 4.16 Warehousing livestock, Mexico

Banco Mercantil del Norte (Martínez, 2006) is a leading Mexican bank which offers a large range of services to its clients. Its inventory programme has an innovative product offered by no other bank in Mexico. The Banorte warehousing facility purchases the crop and then sells it back to the producer at a later date. This service improves client operations by monetizing inventory and providing liquidity as well. It subsequently improves the farmer's balance sheet and offers a contractual guarantee that the crop will be returned to him. Even more on the cutting edge, the Bank has applied this arrangement to shrimp production and, more recently, livestock. Some feel it is too risky because of problems with transporting animals; however, Banorte feels confident that it knows the market and screens clients whose livestock is now being certified.

Source: Martínez (2006)

Financial lease

Another form of using the asset as security is a lease. A lease is a contract between a party that owns an asset (*lessor*) who lets another party (*lessee*) use the asset for a predetermined time in exchange of periodic payments. It is not commonly noted as a type of value chain finance but is included for two reasons. Firstly, it is an alternative financing mechanism for agriculture and secondly, it is similar to many value chain financing instruments in that it separates the use of the asset from the ownership of the asset. For example, in warehouse receipt financing the commodity is used as an asset security without a change of ownership. By not changing ownership unless full payment is made, the asset serves as the collateral. Like value chain financing, this is particularly important when conventional security is not available or sufficient. It is a complimentary alternative finance since, unlike other forms of value chain financing, a lease is used for acquiring fixed assets instead of working capital. The assets that can be used in a lease can be numerous but in relation to agricultural value chain financing, the assets commonly include equipment, warehouses and farm machinery.

In studies by the World Bank a financial lease, which can also be called a lease-purchase agreement, is a viable credit alternative for agricultural equipment and durable assets. A financial lease has four common aspects:

- Amortization of the asset price – includes a purchase option for an agreed amount of payments or at end of lease period.
- Maintenance – lessee is responsible for maintenance and all risks usually associated with ownership without actually owning the asset.
- Non-cancellation – the agreement is generally fixed at the time of the contract (Kloeppinger-Todd, 2007).

A very important aspect of a financial lease is the ease of recovery in case of default on payments. Non-compliance of agreed conditions of payment of maintenance leads to recovery by the owner (leasing company). An application of this instrument in value chain financing is that it provides a collateral

Table 4.5 Financial lease considerations

Client	Leasing company
• Asset serves as collateral.	• Lower transaction costs.
• Lesser credit history may suffice.	• Stronger security: ownership rights versus weaker collateral rights with less costs of repossession.
• May require less down payment.	• Usually more flexible pricing: lease rates not usually regulated.
• May have better prices.	• Less costs of regulatory compliance: lease rates not usually regulated.
• Potential tax-benefits.	• Agricultural leasing can be profitable but may require initial donor/government support.

Source: Kloeppinger-Todd (2007)

alternative, allowing those in a value chain to acquire improved equipment and machinery needed to meet the requirements of competitively producing and processing their products.

Risk mitigation products

> We see very little knowledge or awareness of risk management techniques and price volatility control, such as parametric insurance and options, that could be used to offset some of the risk in agricultural value chains. Experience has shown that there are many ways to reduce risk – information, market knowledge, chain knowledge and/or acquiring links throughout the chain. (Tiffen in Quirós, 2007: 39)

Reducing risk is one of the most critical considerations in finance. These are classified into three types of risk – production, price, and credit (client) risk. The value chain approach helps to reduce price risk through secured markets and sales and production risk through improved access to seeds, farming practices and technology, and agricultural development services. Client risk is also reduced through a better understanding of the client and his/her risks, and through the common use of loan repayments discounted at the point of sale.

Value chain finance also includes many financial and value chain related instruments which are specifically designed to better manage both systemic and individual risks. These instruments, which will be described here include physical tools for product and price risk and financial tools such as insurance and loan guarantees.

Crop/weather insurance

While financing through an agricultural value chain can reduce many procurement, market and repayment risks, its dependence on a single chain can also increase risk when there are external, uncontrollable problems that affect the chain. A most common example is the weather. To a certain extent, the value chain leaders can diversify sources of procurement and markets to reduce risk, but even so, the risks can be significant. An increasingly common form of risk mitigation within the value chain is that of insurance, which is often bundled with other services, namely finance and commodity management. In the large and innovative ICICI bank in India, the insurance services are: 1) weather risk; 2) accident; 3) theft; 4) fire; 5) critical illness; 6) life; 7) motor vehicles; and 8) cash in transit (Hegbe, 2007).

While weather is the most unpredictable and hence most difficult risk to insure, all are important. For example, insurance can mitigate the illness or loss of the farmer or agribusiness leader who is indispensable for the operation of their farm or business can cause the chain to break and losses to follow. For commodities, one of the important roles of a commodity manager is to ensure quality and safety of a product in storage and transit. They provide this assurance not only through careful management and control of the products entrusted to them but also use insurance products to cover their uncontrollable and unforeseen risks.

Despite the difficulties and costs, agricultural weather risk products are growing in importance but, unless subsidized, their overall use is low and there is a reluctance of farmers to voluntarily pay for the insurance. However, others actors farther along the value chain may want to have such insurance and may require it or embed the insurance cost into operational costs. The rationale is clear; if a marketing company has binding sales contracts it is important to have secure procurement. If a crop fails not only will the crop not be available, but neither will the loan repayments for any advances that may have been given. Consequently the funds for purchasing from other producers, if possible, will also be lacking.

Weather risks are very specific to a given value chain and region. For example, too little or too much rain at specific stages of the development of a crop can be disastrous. Since verification of the actual losses of production is very costly, the use of weather insurance products which are indexed to specific weather conditions for determining loss compensation is becoming more popular. Indemnity claims of losses due to abnormal weather events, e.g. excess/ deficit rainfall, hail, are settled based on transparent weather data recorded at meteorological stations, thus reducing the costs of service. A lack of historical data limits the application of this product but specialized institutions, such as the Weather Risk Management Services Company in India, have begun to generate weather data and forecast through a network of sensors to improve the accuracy for those institutions providing indexed insurance services. Even so, weather risk applications in agriculture are not universal, and as noted by its leader, must be linked to an appropriate business model (Agrawal, 2007). Future reading on this topic can be found on the websites of the World Bank and FAO, or those of leading insurance companies active in developing countries.

An example of weather indexed insurance being used in conjunction with value chain financing is shown in BASIX India. In selected commodities, BASIX found that once a pilot model developed with one insurance company, it was quickly replicated by other insurance companies to provide services to 18,000 farmers in the following year (Ramana, 2007b). Even so, the field of indexed insurance is still developing and requires much refining and data history before it can be applied more broadly.

It must be noted that an age-old insurance for production, as well as price risk, is diversification of product lines. While not elaborated on in this volume, diversification is both a factor for those within a chain, as well as for lenders and their portfolios.

Forward contracting

Forward markets, futures options are risk mitigating instruments used in agricultural marketing by producers, investors and traders. Forward contracts obligate the parties to buy or sell a certain amount of product at a future date. Usually, forward contracts are settled between agents who expect to receive or make payments by units of product. The amount of product, date and price parameters (fixed price or method for fixing price at time of sale) are set by the agreement.

One successful programme, using forward contracting of agricultural products, has been developed in Brazil. The rural finance note, called *cedula produto rural* (CPR), was created by the government for loans to agribusinesses and producers. Basically, CPR is a financial asset applied to the value chain to facilitate access to finance. Its mechanism is very simple since the farmer issues a CPR, promising to deliver a given quantity and quality of product at a given future date and locale. In exchange the buyer pays, in advance, a given amount of money corresponding to the quantity of product specified. The unsubsidized loans are backed by the CPR note which commits them to the future product delivery (or to make an equivalent payment). Over US$2.3

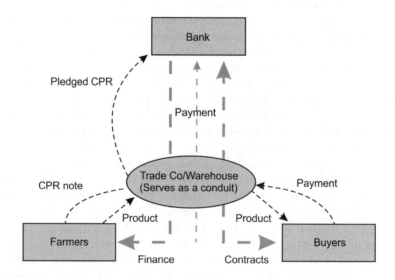

> Farmer signs a CPR (a note pledging the future crop), personal guarantees and/or land in order to finance the crop production.
> Trade Company (Co) takes the CPR and lends to the farmer against it at a discounted rate.
> If the Trade Co is borrowing funds from banks, it will pledge the CPR to those banks.
> Trade Co replaces the CPR with warehouse receipts in order to keep loans with banks.
> When the crop is harvested, the farmer delivers it to the Trade Co which in turn returns the CPR to the farmer.
> Banks perform collateral audits as needed.
> Trade Co sells product to the market and pays the banks.

Figure 4.5 Brazil rural finance note finance
Source: adapted by authors from correspondence with D. Lambright, 2008

billion in financing has been secured by using this forward contracting programme (Alcantara, 2006).

One of the reasons for the growth is that the CPR is a protection against price drops as well as an instrument for accessing production finance. Another important attribute of the CPR is the reduction of risks to the buyers. As stated in the law, CPR is a bond that provides for out-of-court dispute settlements; in other words, the bond guarantees rapid execution in case of breach of contract. This characteristic is a major incentive for the buyers of CPRs, as it reduces risks of moral hazard and it speeds loan recovery when needed.

While the CPR is unique to Brazil, the programme offers a good illustration of how collateral can be transformed as the value chain progresses, since the security begins with the assignment of future receivables, which is then replaced by goods in storage, as the product is moved to warehouses (authors' correspondence with D. Lambright, 2008). Moreover, it is noted that the general use of forward contracts in agriculture is widespread and growing in use. This instrument plays an important role in many of the value chain models.

Introduction of legislative innovation such as the rural product notes in Brazil, that provide access to advance funds on forward contracts and allow for disputes to be rapidly settled in out-of-court dispute settlements, can be considered as an example of increasing access to finance and reducing risks of moral hazard.

Futures

Futures are contracts to trade given amounts of products at a specified date. Futures options provide the holder with the right (but not the obligation) to buy or sell contracts of products at an agreed rate within a period of time, in return for a fee paid to the seller of the option. The use of futures trading is often understood to be a tool for large companies mitigating risks on major commodities. Hedging through the use of futures is a relatively complicated financial process. Most farmers do not understand all the nuances of futures transactions on the commodity exchanges. While it is used primarily by larger companies such as millers and traders, it is found that futures can and often do play an influential role in financing within agricultural value chains. This role is both direct and indirect and can affect producers and agribusinesses of all sizes.

Whereas forward contracts are tailor-made according to the product and involve the expectation of physical delivery or sale transaction of the product at the time specified in the contract, futures are 'packaged' in standardized, readily-tradable contract lots which can be bought and sold by investors through futures exchange markets. The value of futures in finance is two-fold: as a price reference and as an instrument to reduce risk. On one hand, the futures markets' prices are used as a reference for calculating expected returns and for price offerings for future deliveries. This allows both buyers and sellers to have a point of reference, thus leading to less speculation.

The second and foremost value of futures is that they allow traders to hedge (meaning offset or counterbalance), a position established in one market with an opposite obligation or position in another market. For example, a trader can purchase a product for future delivery and simultaneously hedge that purchase with a counterbalancing sale on the futures market. In doing so, it reduces exposure to price risk which not only makes it easier to obtain financing as needed, but also by having price certainty secured allows the buyer of the commodity to offer a better price to the seller. This was noted in the CRDB bank in Tanzania which found that hedging helped coffee producer groups offer a higher purchase price to farmers and gave both banks and borrowers a better ability to manage price risk (Nair, 2007).

A third advantage for futures was noted by Ramana (2007a) who stated that 'the use of commodity derivatives such as futures, not only mitigated commodity price risk but also helped determine cropping patterns based upon futures prices on the exchange platforms'. An example of how this can support both large and small farmers is shown by the MCX Commodity Exchange of India in Box 4.17.

The risk mitigation instruments briefly introduced above are essential to the success of many value chains. These instruments are not needed at all levels of the value chain and some, like futures tend to be used only by larger, more sophisticated traders and agribusinesses but indirectly provide benefits throughout the chain.

It is also important to note that governmental interventions can lessen the interest and need for futures when minimum price levels are set. This is common for some stable commodities in developed countries, such as in the United States, and in developing countries such as India. For example, the government of India has a minimum support price (MSP) for 24 major crops which are announced before the start of the cropping season as a 'safety net'

Box 4.17 Using futures in price risk management, MCX, India

In India, both large and small farmers engage in price hedging following the futures markets. Internet kiosks and point of sale information centres inform farmers and traders of market movements around the globe. The benefits of trading in futures were:

- Prices: futures provide an important clue for choosing the next season's crop.
- Risk management: farmers and traders can hedge on upcoming produce and protect against fall in prices during harvest.
- Warehouse linked risk management: produce procured from farmers can be kept in warehouses and sold in futures market at a suitable lock-in price.
- Collateral financing: a warehouse receipt can be used as collateral by farmers to obtain loans from banks.
- Price dissemination: knowing prices empowers farmers for better negotiation with traders.
- Competition: futures help to create commodity markets which enhance competition, market information and international trade.

Source: Rutten, et al. (2007)

mechanism to help insulate agricultural producers against the unwarranted fluctuations in prices (Ministry of Agriculture, Government of India, 2009). However, such interventions, while reducing risk in the value chain, also reduce the opportunity for growth and development in the use of agricultural futures in the marketplace.

Financial enhancements

Financial enhancements describe a wide range of often complex financing arrangements which are meant to reduce the risk. These include structured financial instruments, guarantees and joint equity investments, among others. In general within financial markets, structured finance instruments reduce the risk of borrower credit-worthiness through 'packaging' of cash flow returns or other receivables which are subject to strict agreements to securitize their repayment. The most critical element of structured finance is the quality of the receivables that form part of the structure finance income streams. Ample evidence of the negative consequences of the aggregation of mixed-quality assets and inadequate supervision and grading are evident in the collapse of the housing mortgage securities market in 2008.

In structured finance in agriculture the performance of the transaction is key and must be carefully evaluated and controlled. Conventional financing may be generally less concerned with the profitability of the transaction but typically the balance sheet of a prospective borrower must be strong. In structured finance the reliance is on the soundness and merits of the transaction (i.e. cash flow or flow of product sales to a buyer) and not the balance sheet. Several of the instruments described earlier may form part of structured finance arrangements.

Within the context of agriculture, it is found that highly complex structuring is not advantageous. Rather, the concept of structured finance is best thought of as 'tailor-designed' finance that uses the concept of market-driven, transaction-secured financing and fits the financing according to the nature of the value chain, its participants and transactions. Other enhancements such as the use of guarantee funds are more widely used to promote agricultural investment and make it more attractive. Joint equity, which can involve public investors can also reduce risk and enhance the acceptability for private investors to finance and/or invest in an agribusiness.

Securitization

Securitization is a financing technique where individual streams of cash flow are bundled and sold on capital markets to investors, many of which are pension funds and managed funds, financial intermediaries and public investors. Securitization has become widespread in the financing of residential housing, automobiles, accounts receivable, commercial properties, and other types of assets. However, it has come under intense scrutiny due to the collapse of the financial markets in 2008 when it was found that many of the securities were made up of poor and mixed quality investments and were misrepresented with high ratings. The lack of proper regulation, oversight and excessive leveraging of securitization has weakened its potential for widespread use in the near future.

Despite the problems stemming from mismanagement of securities indicated above, there are examples of its effective use in agricultural value chain financing as well as in microfinance and development finance. The potential for the use of securitization in agriculture is limited to commodities and products that can be readily bundled into packages of nearly identical products, which can be traded on commodity exchanges. An example is fattening cattle in Colombia where the livestock sector was hindered by the high cost and processes for obtaining conventional commercial financing. Through an innovative approach, the National Agriculture and Livestock Exchange (BNA) developed a scheme under which securities of cattle were able to be listed and sold on Colombia's stock and security exchanges, as described in Box 4.18, to raise funds for the feeding of livestock. These are then traded on an exchange, which also provides supervision over the entire process and all those involved.

Box 4.18 Livestock securitization, BNA, Colombia

There is a tradition in the use of securitization structures in the livestock production sector in Colombia, with the National Agriculture and Livestock Exchange (BNA) playing a lead role. To increase financing flows to the livestock sector, the BNA developed a scheme under which a Trust was set up to take ownership of unfattened calves and the pasturelands where the livestock is fattened. The BNA was responsible for selecting farmers to participate in the scheme against a strict set of criteria and the selected farmers received finance from the Trust to purchase animal feed.

The Trust issued securities on Colombia's stock and security exchanges, at rates which were determined by competition among the country's institutional investors and this competition ensured that the farmers in the scheme were faced with reasonable interest charges. The ranchers fatten the animals for 11 months and at the end of the period the calves are sold by the firm operating the process to pay the liabilities acquired with the investors, with the remaining earnings payable to the ranchers. The scheme is based essentially on repossession (repo) arrangements, with ownership being transferred back to the ranchers at the end of the fattening period and the marketing agent selling the cattle into the market on behalf of the ranchers.

Key elements in the scheme's success were the availability of a developed stock and security market, sophisticated investors, technical support and regular inspection by an independent agency to ensure standards were maintained and the use of insurance to mitigate risk for investors. Several iterations of the scheme were carried out by the BNA in the early 2000s, resulting in tens of millions of dollars being raised for livestock farmers.

Source: UNCTAD Secretariat (2002)

Loan guarantees

Loan guarantees have been used in agricultural finance in many countries. Their overall use has often been associated with considerable subsidies as a result of high payouts in relation to the income generated and due to their costs of operation. When guarantees are used within value chain financing, the chain linkages and close interaction and knowledge of the different parties involved increases the opportunities for their successful application. The following two examples display their use at the lower and upper end of the value chain.

In Mexico, FIRA, a second tier agricultural bank, provides funds and guarantees to support agriculture and the rural sector. It works with para-finance agents to manage the funds and guarantees of farmers who would otherwise not qualify for loans from banks. These para-agents are companies and individuals, such as agribusinesses, processors and farmer unions, who have commercial relationships with the producers. They select final credit recipients and manage the loans to the farmers and guarantees with the bank.

An example is shown in Figure 4.6, with the Regional Agricultural Union of Producers (UNIPRO). First, UNIPRO, acting as a para-finance agent, contacts FIRA to negotiate a line of credit which is disbursed through a first tier bank. It then contacts the bank that will disburse the money and FIRA signs over to the bank the resources it will be lending to the agent. The bank then dispenses the money and UNIPRO distributes it to the beneficiaries. FIRA gives the bank a guarantee and charges the costs to UNIPRO. The risk is shared. A group of members of UNIPRO provide partial collateral as a guarantee for the money and are required to set up a trust fund with contributions from the farmer and the producer organization for 30 per cent of the total credit as a liquid guarantee. The bank also carries 30 per cent of the risk of the operation. When the producer repays the loan, UNIPRO pays the bank and the bank returns the money to FIRA. The trust fund returns the Union's contribution, and the Union returns the amount paid in by the producers.

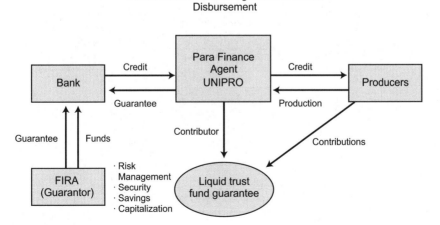

Figure 4.6 Para-finance guarantees in Mexico
Source: Chávez (2006)

The UNIPRO model involves multiple guarantees: the bank has loan guarantees from FIRA and UNIPRO, UNIPRO in turn has a partial farmer trust fund guarantee and a partial bank shared guarantee, and in addition, much of the production is guaranteed through contract farming agreements with a major warehouse.

In a different model on a more macro level, Rabobank manages a loan guarantee fund to enhance the eligibility of farmers, agribusinesses and traders requiring financing. In addition to sales contracts, warehouse receipts and/or other types of conventional and value chain collateral, it is found that a partial guarantee can assist in making financing more readily available and often at a lower cost. As shown in Figure 4.7 in the case of the Sustainable Agricultural Guarantee Fund created for developing countries, public sector agencies may be involved in order to attract the investment of the private sector.

In addition to helping attract investment, guarantees may be needed to restore finance and investment. In late 2008, the global financial crisis affected the availability of finance for trade, prompting the International Finance Corporation (IFC) of the World Bank group to significantly increase its global finance programme by providing guarantees that cover the payment risk in trade transactions with local banks in emerging countries. It found that the demand for trade-related risk mitigation increased significantly as a result of the global financial crisis (IFC, 2009).

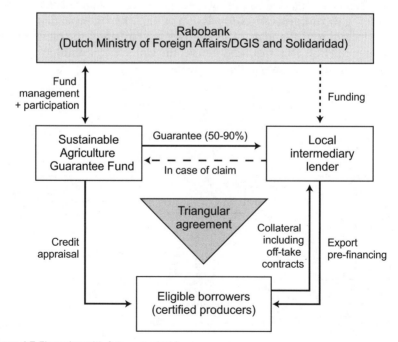

Figure 4.7 Financing with future receivables
Source: Wortelboer (2007)

Joint ventures

In order to increase investment and value addition in agriculture and agribusiness, much direct capital investment is required from equity investors into the value chains. Much of this is done directly by investors and owners within the chain but there is an increasing interest in specialized funds for investment. In Africa, the Actis Africa Agribusiness Fund, for example, invests in equity and quasi-equity in selected sectors. The Actis strategy is to 'participate across value chain' in activities related to production and processing of, and services related to (i.e. inputs, logistics, distribution and marketing), biological products, plant or animal, whether for food or non-food purposes. Critical success factors noted for investment include:

- Investment in value addition, market led, established businesses in free markets.
- Experienced sector specific and focused management team at fund level.
- Rigorous application of the fund's investment and decision making process (Actis, 2007).

Box 4.19 Public–private contract farming, Thailand

Samutsongkhram and Samutsakorn provinces are shrimp producing areas in Thailand. A collaborative partnership among various public and private stakeholders works to enable shrimp farmers to revive and secure marine farming with sustainable aquaculture practices. The value chain involves numerous players with a range of roles, at the heart of which is a contract farming arrangement and supporting technical services:

- The Ta Chin Shrimp Farmers' Cooperative selects participating farmers according to the cooperative's principles and project requirements; manages contract farming of products to be forwarded by the cooperative members; prepares shrimp farm plans; trains the participating farmers on shrimp culture technology and standards; coordinates adequate and timely financial sources for farmers; and arranges for a traceable shrimp production system.
- The Bank for Agriculture and Agricultural Cooperatives (BAAC) provides credit services for shrimp culture.
- The provincial fisheries offices promote shrimp culture businesses and careers that adhere to the food safety standards and provide technology and certification.
- The Coastal Fisheries Research and Development monitors food safety and certifies the sanitary conditions of the marine products aimed for export.
- The Coastal Aquaculture Station transfers technology for commercial marine shrimp culture and diagnoses disease amongst marine shrimp.
- The Ministry provides capacity building to the cooperatives in business management and technology.
- The Provincial Commerce Offices support marketing of the shrimp.
- The Agricultural Marketing Cooperatives provide inputs and marine shrimp feed.
- Pac Food Co., Ltd. and Union Frozen Products Co., Ltd. purchase shrimp produced according to the contract farming agreement made with the Cooperative.
- Participating Shrimp farmers produce shrimp according to the regulations and requirements.

Source: Prasittipayong (2007)

Public–private partnerships. Public–private partnerships can provide a solid foundation to deal with the complexity of certain value chains – dividing areas of responsibility according to core competencies, resources and mission. The case of shrimp farming in Thailand shown in Box 4.19 describes how contract farming is an integral element in a sector with many interrelated public and private sector components.

Figure 4.8 illustrates the flow of finance within the shrimp industry value chain in Thailand. The use of contracts between producers and the cooperative, as well as technical assistance to ensure quality and sustainability are key consideration to BAAC in order to provide financing for the small-scale shrimp farmers.

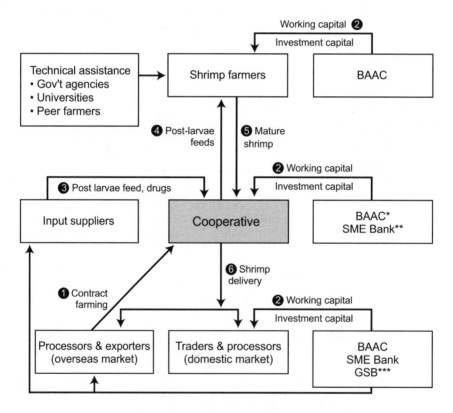

* Bank for Agriculture and Agricultural Cooperatives
** Small and Medium Enterprise Development Bank of Thailand
*** Government Savings Bank

Figure 4.8 Value chain financing: shrimp industry model
Source: Prasittipayong in Digal (2009: 108)

Bringing it together

The agricultural value chain finance mechanisms and tools were presented singularly in this chapter to highlight their characteristics and uses. However, these are often used in combination and for this reason larger financial institutions specializing in financing agriculture offer an array of conventional and unconventional financial tools and options, such as transactional-based finance instruments. A sample of the agricultural value chain finance instruments offered by Standard Charter Bank in Africa is illustrated in Figure 4.9.

As noted, various financial instruments are used to finance the processes as the products move through the value chain. In addition, financing in turn flows from the direct recipients to others in the chain through other instruments as described earlier. A summary of the principal benefits and limitations and how they can be applied is shown in Table 4.6.

Standard Charter Bank value chain finance instruments

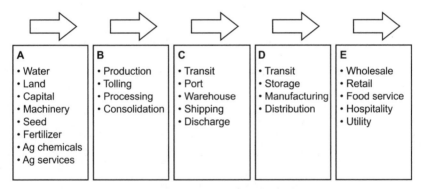

A	B	C	D	E
• Water	• Production	• Transit	• Transit	• Wholesale
• Land	• Tolling	• Port	• Storage	• Retail
• Capital	• Processing	• Warehouse	• Manufacturing	• Food service
• Machinery	• Consolidation	• Shipping	• Distribution	• Hospitality
• Seed		• Discharge		• Utility
• Fertilizer				
• Ag chemicals				
• Ag services				

A • Grain hedge, fertilizer hedge, working capital, project finance, structured finance, term debt.

B • Pre-finance, working capital.

C • SPV – special purpose vehicles, repurchase agreements, warehouse inventory.

D • Structured receivable financing.

E • Debtor finance, working capital, foreign exchange, derivatives, term debt.

Figure 4.9 Capturing the agri-food value chain
Source: Muiruri (2007)

Table 4.6 Summary analysis of agricultural value chain finance products

Instrument	Benefits	Limitations	Application potential
A. Product financing			
1. Trader credit	• Farm-gate finance with ease of transaction. • Culturally accepted and well known at all levels. • Secures sale/purchase and price of seller and buyer.	• Non-transparency of true market value. • Often informal with potential for side-selling. • Quality and quantity uncertain when given pre-harvest.	• 'Middleman' traders will remain important but as chains integrate will lessen in importance. • Tendency of traders towards acting as agents of wholesalers.
2. Input supplier credit	• Buyers obtain needed inputs. • Suppliers secure sales.	• Input costs may be excessive. • Lack of security in repayment. • Lack of competitive suppliers in many regions.	• Focus on reducing administration and risk with multi-party links with banks; produce buyers are promising for direct payments from sale. • Quality and safety are growing concerns.
3. Marketing company credit	• Secures quantity and price. • Funds advanced as needed; payments often discounted directly. • Eliminates need for trader. • Contract terms for finance, price and product specs.	• May not be directly accessible to small farmers. • Credit advances increase financial outlay and administration. • Compliance of contracts is often not respected.	• Value chain control through contract farming is growing in importance. • Value chain approaches reduce transaction costs and risks.
4. Lead firm financing	• Secures market and price. • Technical guidance for higher yields and quality. • Less side-selling options due to closer monitoring. • Enforceable contracts reduce side-selling. • Lead firm can often hedge price risk.	• Less access for small farmers. • Restricts price rise gains to producer. • Cost of management and enforcement of contracts.	• Growing use and strong potential to provide access to markets, technical assistance and credit.

Instrument	Benefits	Limitations	Application potential
B. Receivables financing			
5. Trade receivables finance	• Reduces finance constraints for exporters and eases repayment urgency from importers. • Can be cheaper than bank loan alternatives.	• Requires a proven track record. • Not suitable for perishable products. • Is most suitable for large transactions.	• Is used for import-export transactions by companies for major commodities. • Increasingly used for input suppliers, equipment dealers and major commodities.
6. Factoring	• Provides a means of capital for operations. • Facilitates international business and finance by passing collection risk to a third party factor.	• Complex and requires a factoring agency, which is only an option for some countries and commodities. • Lack of knowledge and interest by financial markets.	• Less common but is growing in use in agriculture for processors and input suppliers where product flows and accounts are stable.
7. Forfaiting	• Like factoring, it frees up capital to be used elsewhere in the business and takes care of collection risks and costs. • Can be selectively used for specific accounts.	• Forfaiting requires selling the accounts at a discount. • Complex and requires the presence of specialized agencies.	• Less common but similar to factoring. • Invoice instruments are negotiable but complex, limiting their application potential.
C. Physical asset collateralization			
8. Warehouse receipts	• Uses inventory as collateral to increase access to financing. • Where organization and trust are built, can also work on a less formal basis without the official WR legislation in place.	• Commodity traded must be well standardized by type, grade and quality. • Increases costs. • Often requires special legislation.	• Common and used at all levels with high interest and growth potential. • Currently is used for durable commodities but with increased processing and improved storage, the range of use can expand.
9. Repurchase agreements (repos)	• Can reduce financial costs and has proven successful in selected commodities with well functioning commodity exchanges.	• Complex and requires commodities to be stored with accredited collateral managers and requires commodity exchanges.	• Limited potential in near future and used infrequently by exporters for some commodities.

Instrument	Benefits	Limitations	Application potential
10. Financial leasing (lease-purchase)	• Allows more loan security and ease of asset repossession in case of default. • Especially good where legal system for loan collection is weak. • Often tax benefits.	• Requires coordination of seller, buyer and financier. • Only feasible for medium to long-term purchases of non-perishables. • Often requires insurance.	• High potential use for equipment if legislation allows.

D. Risk mitigation products

Instrument	Benefits	Limitations	Application potential
11. Insurance	• Reduces risk for all parties in value chain. • Commonly used and easily applied for fire, vehicles, health and death insurance. • Crop and livestock insurance is increasing.	• Costly, requiring subsidy, when applied to agricultural production. • Insufficient data limits weather indexing use in insurance.	• High interest by many donors and governments increasing use. • Growth without subsidies will be modest for production insurance until sufficient risk data is available.
12. Forward contracts	• Companies can hedge price risk, thus lowering financial risk and cost. • Can be used as collateral for borrowing. • Not dependent upon commodity exchanges. • Benefits can flow though chain when one party forward contracts and can offer forward or fixed prices to others.	• Requires reliable market information. • Commodity traded must be well standardized by type, grade and quality.	• Frequently used by larger companies and for major commodities. • Potential to increase significantly wherever reliable market information is available.
13. Futures	• Used globally in agricultural commodities to hedge risk. • Futures serve as price benchmarks for reference trade.	• Commodity traded must be well standardized by type, grade and quality. • Requires a well organized futures market.	• Growing use and potential in countries with functioning commodity exchanges. • Use is limited to large producers, processors and marketing companies.

Instrument	Benefits	Limitations	Application potential
F. Financial enhancements			
14. Securitization instruments	• Potential to reach lower-cost capital market funding where homogeneous pooling is possible. • Successfully used in microfinance.	• Costly and complex to set up. • Adversely affected by securitization problems from the sub-prime financial crisis.	• Limited potential for agricultural value chain investments of similar tenor and cash flow.
15. Loan guarantees	• Finance risk reduced and/or the business venture creates more access for funding. • Can facilitate investment needed in a value chain.	• Costly and often subsidized in agriculture. • Can reduce lender responsibility and accountability.	• Occasionally used as incentive for stimulating capital flows to infrastructure, new markets and exports and occasionally production.
16. Joint venture finance	• Provides equity capital and borrowing capacity. • Reduces financial leverage risk of investors. • Often brings expertise and/or markets.	• Hard to attract suitable investors of common vision. • Dilutes investor returns. • Hard for small producers to participate.	• Growing potential in globalizing world. • Strategic partnership, including public and private, is increasingly important in value chains.

Introduction to Case Studies

Chapter 4 describes and Table 4.6 summarizes the many instruments that are available in value chain financing. Some of them require relatively high levels of sophistication, chain integration and/or enabling conditions, yet, this need not be the case.

The chapter includes two case studies – one from Niger, and a second from Central America – that illustrate the different levels of complexity that may exist when financial instruments are utilized in the development of a value chain. The first case study from Niger illustrates an application of one instrument, warehouse receipts, with very small farmers. The second case study offers a view of a complex, integrated financial and value chain system in Central America that integrates value chains from the start to finish, involving many value chain financing products and services.

Case Study 2. Producer-driven financing of farm inputs: Niger informal inventory credit

Emmanuelle LeCourtois, Agribusiness Development Consultant, FAO, and Ake Olofsson, Rural Finance Program Officer, FAO

Introduction

Warehouse receipt financing, also called inventory credit, is borrowing money against a stock of commodities stored in a warehouse as loan guarantee. It is a common financing mechanism, most often used by larger traders. In addition to the owner of the produce and a lending institution, the mechanism normally also involves a warehouse manager. The warehouse manager issues a receipt that is a document that provides proof of ownership of the stored commodities. Most warehouse receipts are issued in negotiable form, making them eligible as collateral for loans and allowing transfer of ownership without having to deliver the physical commodity. The mechanism is known to require special governmental policies and regulations, often involving specialized commodity management agencies, but as shown in this case, can be applied at the community level.

Various different approaches to inventory credit exist. In most cases, the operation is a triangular arrangement between a bank, a borrower and a warehouse operator/manager. The borrower can be a trader, a miller, a large farmer or a group of farmers. A crucial element of inventory credit is the availability of reliable storage facilities and storage managers/operators. The latter should not only possess the required infrastructure and technical skills in storage management and pest control, but should also have business skills and be independent from political pressure, which will provide a reasonable guarantee of the integrity of the stocks.

Inventory credit is seldom used directly by producers. This case study shows how it can be applied successfully in a relatively informal manner by building upon the capacity of producer organizations and local financial institutions.

Background

In 1999, the Food and Agriculture Organization of the United Nations (FAO), through its project 'Promotion of the Use of Agricultural Inputs by Producer Organizations', developed and introduced an inventory credit model (*crédit warranté*) in Niger in which farmers, through their associations, obtain short-term credit from local financial institutions by storing part of their harvest as a guarantee for a loan. The immediate objective was to respond to the lack of access to short-term credit for the purchase of agricultural inputs, mainly fertilizers. Today, the model has gained a widespread recognition and is considered by farmers' organizations, financial institutions and development partners alike, as an effective tool that can help improve food security and thereby also reduce poverty in rural areas.

Small-scale producers in Niger usually lack assets and financial resources and, in order to satisfy immediate cash needs, often have to sell off their produce immediately after harvest. Sales made at harvest, when prices normally are at their lowest, means that they receive less revenue, which in turn impedes on their capacity to purchase inputs, especially high quality fertilizers and seeds needed for the next cropping season. Fixed assets being the main form of collateral acceptable to banks, farmers are normally not able to obtain seasonal credit that would help them purchase the required inputs. The soil in Niger being generally poor and the country being regularly struck by drought, means that appropriate use of quality inputs is particularly important in order to increase agricultural production.

A cycle of poverty in Niger is shown in Figure 4.10. In order to break this vicious circle of low yields, low output prices, low revenues and insufficient use of inputs, and in the extension also to improve the local food security situation, the project contemplated a mechanism whereby credit could be obtained against the deposit of agricultural produce likely to increase substantially in value over a short period of time. The repayment capacity of the farmers would thus be linked with the marketing and sale of agricultural produce at a time when prices were more advantageous for the farmers.

The development of the inventory credit model was closely linked to, and also dependent upon, other activities, in particular the organization of farmers into producer associations in order to offer them a stronger position when negotiating price and quantity with input suppliers and the promotion of a correct use of fertilizers. The latter was done in close collaboration with the

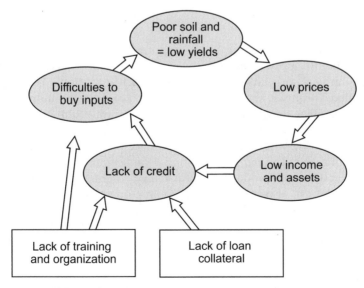

Figure 4.10 Poverty production cycle
Source: case authors, LeCourtois and Olofsson

International Crops Research Institute for the Semi-Arid Tropics (ICRISAT) that successfully experimented with adequate and, at the same time, affordable doses of fertilizers. The FAO provided technical support, essential training and capacity building to the farmers and their associations and to the participating local banks.

The development of the inventory credit model originates from the need to improve and strengthen the stake of producers in the agricultural inputs value chain. The main objective of the FAO project was to identify and test innovative mechanisms that would support the promotion of agricultural inputs usage, in particular fertilizers, by farmers and their organizations, and to establish technical and economic standards that would guarantee the appropriateness/reproducibility/durability of the application of inputs. This is to assist the various actors along the value chain in the elaboration of a national level strategy, built in partnership, for improved farm input supply in support of a more sustainable agriculture. Another objective was to contribute to reducing poverty and food insecurity in the country by increasing productivity and improving storage facilities.

The project also created a limited number of input stores managed by farmer associations. These input stores would guarantee the availability of quality inputs at the time they are needed. The sale of inputs is done on a cash basis since the farmers' organizations are not set up for managing sales on credit. Storage infrastructure, existing or new, was offered to the producer associations as a grant from the government or other development projects. In the case of construction of new storage facilities, farmer associations contributed with labour.

The inventory credit model

In Niger, in order to respond to the opportunities and constraints of the country, the inventory credit model was adapted to be undertaken directly between farmers' associations and local financial institutions. The first step in this model begins at harvest time, when the farmers' associations ask their members to define the quantities of their produce they would want to deposit in a warehouse as a guarantee for a bank loan. In some cases, the farmer associations themselves also store their own produce when they have conditions which permit this. The farmers and their organizations in Niger are able to store dry and durable products, such as millet, sorghum and beans, and to a lesser extent can also store some vegetable products such as potatoes and onions. They are interested in storing products that are subject to seasonal surplus and that show a positive price evolution over a short period of time.

The next step is for the associations to contact a local financial institution in order to discuss the total loan amount available to them and match this against the total potential stock. Adjustments are normally needed since the potential stock often exceeds the financing capacity of the local bank. A loan agreement is then signed with the bank and the association distributes the total loan among the members in proportion with the relative volume stored by each farmer. The farmers are responsible to their association and the association, not the individual farmer, is responsible to the financial institution. This significantly lowers the transaction costs and risk for the financial institution.

After agreements have been reached, the produce from the association is deposited in a safe and reliable warehouse or storage space where it remains during the duration of the loan. Once stored, the financial institution and the producer association jointly carry out a quality control of both the stock and the warehouse, making sure that the stock is safe and free from contamination or insects. The warehouse is then closed with two padlocks: one for the producers' organization and one for the bank, so that neither of the parties can open it without the other one being present. During the period of storage, the two parties carry out regular controls of the storage facility and the stored produce.

At the expiration of the loan, the stock is sold at a price higher than that at the harvest time, thus enabling the borrower to repay his/her outstanding debt and to make a profit from the operation. Experience shows that stock value tends to increase by 30 to 40 per cent 4 to 6 months after harvest when it is released from the warehouse as indicated in Table 4.7.

Similar to the distribution process of the loans, the producer association acts on behalf of its members and collects repayments from each individual and transfers them in bulk to the local financial institution. The bank maintains the right to the stock until the settlement of the outstanding debt and can in theory seize the produce and sell it to a third party. The experiences in Niger have however shown that many producers who have used parts of their loans to finance other income generating activities that in turn have rendered profit, have been able to pay back the loan without having to use the income from the sale of the stock.

The local banks normally grant credit up to 60 to 80 per cent of stock value at harvest time (at low prices). Usually, the farmers use the loan to carry out income generating activities such as petty trade, processing, marketing of other products, etc. As pointed out earlier, this extra revenue often allows farmers to reimburse their loans.

Table 4.7 Price increase gained from inventory credit

Year	November harvest price (CFA/kg)	Price after six months	Percentage increase
1	50	175	250%
2	50	100	100%
3	100	245	145%
4	110	170	55%
5	150	200	33%

Source: FAO (2009)

Current situation

While not yet reaching national levels, the results in Niger show a rapid increase of loans granted, as well as a wealth increase among small-scale farmers as they use the borrowed money to finance income generating activities. At the moment, the resources and business capacity of the local financial institutions are very weak which limits them from supporting an expansion of the system. As with any type of credit, inventory credit also requires financially secure local banks with a high level of management capacity.

The relationship between the number of beneficiaries and the total number of rural families, i.e. the penetration rate, went from 3 per cent in 2001 to 5.3 per cent in 2004, involving:

- 129 local financial institutions;
- 104,741 clients;
- 1,970,881 families.

From 1999 to 2006, it can be concluded that:

- There has been a strong interest in the use of inventory credit from producers and their organizations, development projects and local financial institutions.
- The repayment has been excellent with rates reaching 100 per cent.
- A lack of resources has prevented local banks from responding fully to the strong demand for this type of financing mechanism. It is estimated that only 50 per cent of total loan requests were satisfied.
- Interest in inventory credit was very high – growing in initial years (1999 to 2003) from zero to CFA 180 million, and then to approximately CFA 1 trillion by 2006. (FAO, 2009)

Implementation of the inventory credit model was based upon a partnership between development organizations (FAO, International Fund for Agricultural Development (IFAD), and others), ICRISAT, and local financial institutions. In order to respond to the requirements of a supportive legal regulatory framework, the monetary authorities, i.e. the Central Bank, were involved at an early stage of the planning. It is important to note that the Central Bank has since officially recognized and legally accepted stock of agricultural produce as guarantee for loans by financial institutions.

Results

According to the goals, several results, effects and impacts have been observed. For the producer and the farmers' association, the economic results of the inventory credit (averaged over several years and different types of products stored and varied types of additional income generating activities made possible from the loans obtained) have shown a 25 per cent average increase of the value of the stored produce, a net profit of 8 per cent on the additional income generating activities, i.e. a total increase (net of all costs) of approximately 33 per cent of the capital in 4–6 months. Other studies also show that on average 20 per cent of the gross margin is being spent on agricultural inputs. On average, 12 per cent of the loans obtained were used to purchase inputs and 16 per cent of the value of the stored produce was used to purchase inputs. On average, the use of the stored produce consisted of: seeds (29 per cent), to bridge gaps in food items between harvesting periods (18 per cent), and for sale (53 per cent). Studies carried out by CARE International and ICRISAT further confirm that part of the extra income generated from activities financed with the inventory credit loans is also used to purchase agricultural inputs.

At the financial level, inventory credit has enabled the local rural financial institutions to increase their loan portfolio and to reduce their credit risk by obtaining a tangible guarantee that is easy to divide and to realize, adding to this the positive effects of solidarity guarantee and lower cost, by grouping small loans into one for which the farmers' associations take responsibility. In the longer perspective, inventory credit may increase the supply of financial services to rural households by attracting new financial operators to establish themselves in the rural areas and by offering more services, in particular savings and deposits as the farm revenues increase. As of 2009, the loans granted under the inventory credit model have been 100 per cent repaid with interest without experiencing significant difficulties. This has also been important in improving the health of the lending portfolios of the rural financial institutions and increases their credibility/eligibility towards the banking sector for accessing lines of credit for their operations.

Key issues and constraints

The main current constraint in Niger is the limited capacity, both in terms of resources and management, of the participating local financial institutions. Expanding the Niger experience by offering additional external resources could seriously damage, even destroy, the system if the management capacity of the local financial institutions is not simultaneously increased.

As shown in Figure 4.11, the farmers' associations hold a crucial position in the process. They are the link that allows both collection of produce into one centralized place and the distribution of the bulk loan from the local financial institution to the farmers in accordance with the quantities stored by each of them. It also plays an important role in capacity building and supports the farmers in their decision making. In deciding what quantities a producer will store, it is very important that he/she understands the proper financial situation and the mechanisms that regulate the revenues. It is also important for the individual to understand the concepts of cash-flow and savings and to forecast the costs, prices, profit margins and self-financing, in order to plan and take correct decisions.

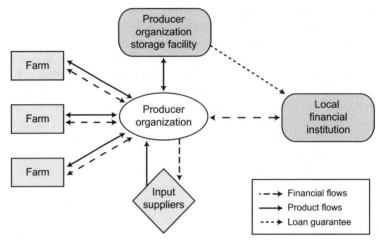

Figure 4.11 Inventory credit flow chart
Source: case authors, LeCourtois and Olofsson

Lessons learned

Since its implementation in Niger in 1999, the inventory credit system has significantly contributed to reduce rural poverty. Because it enables farmers to increase the use of quality agricultural inputs, the system has resulted in a significant increase of yields, thereby contributing to food security in the rural areas. In Niger, inventory credit is thus playing a key role in the fulfilment of the United Nation's Millennium Development Goal No. 1 ('eradicate extreme poverty and hunger').

The viability of the system, a guarantee for its duration and development, depends on the interest and advantages that the stakeholders (farmers and their associations, rural financial institutions, development projects, NGOs, government, donors) find therein (profit, new types of loan guarantees, food security, securitization/finance of agricultural cycles, release from debt/impoverishment, etc.). It is also determined by the willingness, commitment and the intrinsic ability of these actors to reinforce their own capacity and that of others in order to improve the professionalism at all levels.

In summary, the following lessons for application can be drawn from the experience in Niger:

- Establishing reliable producer organizations and building their capacity to become important actors in the input supply and output marketing chains is the foundation for success.
- Working with local financial institutions who are close to farmers favours feelings of partnership and ownership of the model.
- Well managed resources and strong local financial institutions are key to expansion.
- Uncontrolled food aid may distort market prices on stored produce and lower the repayment capacity of the farmers.

- Longer-term impact on food security is possible but studies would need to be carried out in order to determine the optimal levels of stored produce at local, national and regional levels and the possibilities of enabling efficient transfer of produce from surplus to deficit areas.
- Inventory credit is one way of using the value chain for offering short-term credit; it is not a panacea for the lack of financial services in rural areas. Longer term loans for investment in agriculture would still require other systems.
- The development process takes time; development agencies and policy-makers tend to want to move too fast in extending the model, thereby endangering its existence and durability.

Replication

Replication of the system in other regions and countries requires:

- Understanding the setting, the organizations and the market conditions and trends.
- Agricultural products that can be stored for a period of 6 to 9 months without deterioration of quality.
- A strong, positive price evolution on the market (local, national or regional) from harvest time to 6 to 12 months later.
- The existence of adequate warehouse infrastructures.
- The capacity of farmers to produce a surplus of agricultural products that can be subject to storage.
- A sufficient level of organization among producers and measures to reinforce it.
- A correct assessment of the inputs procurement value chain, and in particular fertilizers, in terms of availability, quality and price, as well as the identification of support measures that would allow farmers to manage their use and distribution more efficiently.

Because the inventory credit inventory credit model has shown its effectiveness in reducing poverty in rural areas in Niger, it has been selected as an example of 'good practice' being implemented at a regional level in Niger, Burkina Faso, Mali and Senegal under a FAO/Belgium multilateral cooperation programme. The experiences in Niger also continue to expand and inventory credit forms part of a programme focusing on the establishment of *boutiques d'intrants*, or farm input stores, run by the farmers' associations, thus building on the experiences of the previous project in this area.

Case references

Coulter, J. and Shepherd, A. (1995) 'Inventory credit: an approach to developing agricultural markets', *FAO Agricultural Services Bulletin No. 120*, Rome.

FAO (2009) Project GCP/NER/041/BEL, http://www.fao.org/landandwater/fieldpro/niger/default_fr.htm [accessed 4 October 2009].

Case Study 3. LAFISE Group: integrated financial instruments and value chain services

Enrique Zamora, General Manager of LAFISE Agropecuaria, and Calvin Miller

Introduction

The LAFISE Group in Central America plays a role at every stage of the value chain through an integrated system of financial services and agricultural value chain addition, including processing, commodity management, and national and export marketing. LAFISE, headquartered in Nicaragua has a *Bancentro* banking network comprised of banks and financial services in 10 countries in Latin America and the United States, and four associated group companies – Agropecuaria LAFISE (agriculture), Almacenadora LAFISE (storage and commodity management), Seguros LAFISE (insurance) and LAFISE Trade. It also works directly with governmental organizations and NGOs in order to provide the services needed to meet the needs of the participants in the value chain, with a special emphasis given to small-scale farmers.

Overview

Nicaragua is an agricultural country with the second lowest per capita income level in Latin America. With a history of conflict, wide political shifts and interference, and an unstable currency, investment and lending through conventional sources has been low. This is much more aggravated in agriculture where rural infrastructure is weak, systemic climatic risks such as hurricanes are high and political interference in prices and interest rates have been common. In addition, agricultural producers operate on a small scale without strong organizations.

Nicaragua has the potential to be highly competitive in the marketplace with a number of agricultural chains, including fruit, coffee, basic grains and milk and livestock. With the opening of free trade agreements in the region, both the opportunity for growth and the increased threat of international competition heightened the need to create effective value chains in the agricultural sector of Nicaragua. However, in order to do so, it required organization, training and investment at multiple levels. Critical areas requiring attention were:

- dispersed production with small volumes;
- poor product handling and post-harvest practices;
- need for transport, storage, processing and packaging;
- lack of and informality of markets, without price and market information;
- price distortions;
- need for financing at all levels.

Agricultural chain cost distribution

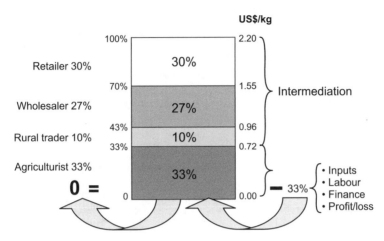

Figure 4.12 Traditional cost structure in Nicaragua
Source: case authors, Zamora and Miller

As shown in Figure 4.12, the traditional intermediation expenses and costs of financing in Nicaragua were too high as the process was inefficient and returns to the farmers were low. Under such conditions, LAFISE realized that directly financing smallholder farmers in the existing system of production and marketing was not viable – the chains must be organized, shortened and modernized.

LAFISE was well placed to provide comprehensive support to the agricultural value chain. With financial resources from its Bancentro banking network, established in Nicaragua in 1991, it had both the financing resources and an international presence with considerable experience in capital markets, international finance and other commercial banking instruments. With the creation of an agribusiness company, Agropecuaria LAFISE, it could begin to both improve and increase its lending to the sector, but also profitably begin to diversify its activities, its direct knowledge of specific value chains and open the door to provision of additional financial services.

Working directly with small-scale producers requires more than financing and market linkages. Agropecuaria LAFISE was quick to understand the importance of collaboration with both governmental and NGOs to support their work in providing the technical and organizational training and capacity building needed to be able to meet the requirements of the firm. Formal and/or informal collaborative agreements are developed with the social and/ or technical organizations and universities in a region or sector for provision of services complementary to those of the agricultural company.

For mutual benefit, the goal of LAFISE is to convert traditional agricultural producers into rural entrepreneurs who have the capacity and commitment

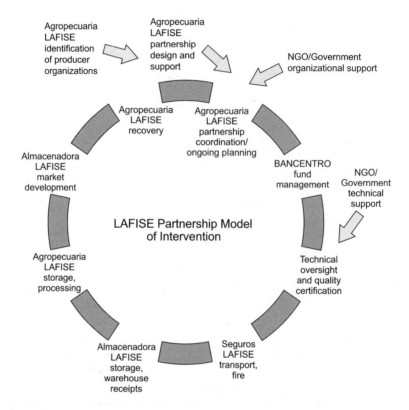

Figure 4.13 LAFISE Group partner model of intervention
Source: case authors, Zamora and Miller

of market oriented, commercial agriculture. In doing so, currently with over 5,000 small-scale producers, it benefits both the farmers and its companies with higher returns, increased investment and more security in each other's operations. By working together in all phases of production, marketing and financing, it strives to shorten the chain between growers and consumers and achieve its motto of a 'win–win' relationship. LAFISE Group support begins as soon as farmers receive their production loans and continues until they have collected the proceeds on their overseas product sales. It includes access to the office in Miami, which is responsible for visiting trade fairs and identifying buyers. As soon as a good potential buyer has been identified, paperwork is simple. The presence of Agropecuaria LAFISE helps to assure the buyer as to product quality and speeds up operations and safeguards collection for the seller.

As shown in Figure 4.13, the principal company for agricultural value chains is the Agropecuaria LAFISE. It plays the central role as initiator, organizer and coordinator of the producers throughout the process, including that of technical assistance, value addition and payment. This company works in

LAFISE Group Integrated Service Model

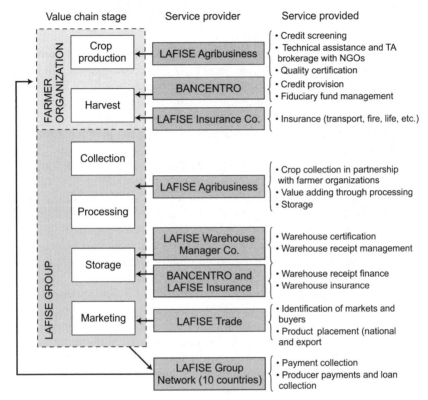

Figure 4.14 LAFISE Group integrated service model
Source: case authors Zamorra and Miller

multiple chains, including dairy, beans, plantains, honey and coffee. These include value chains in agriculture, livestock and agro-industry. In some agricultural chains, such as dairy, it offers the whole range of services from provision of inputs, collection, processing, packaging, wholesaling and retailing. In pineapples its value added includes exporting and selling through its partner company LAFISE Trade. In such chains, it is active in all aspects except for production. Through its partners it is also active with microenterprises, housing, commerce and other non-agricultural activities which also can benefit those with whom it works in the agricultural chains.

As shown in Figure 4.14, there are many specific service provision aspects of the work. The LAFISE Group is involved in undertaking the processes at all stages of the post-harvest and value addition, but the farmers, with their organizations, and often with technical assistance support from partnering development organizations, are responsible for the production and harvest.

LAFISE Group operates many different kinds of support arrangements for agricultural value chains, from an array of financial products (credit and otherwise) to technical assistance and marketing services. Some of these are listed below:

1. *Commodity Management and Warehousing.* LAFISE owns a warehouse operation in Nicaragua where farmers can store their crops. They can either store their full crop or receive a down payment for a maximum of 70 per cent of the value, which is paid within two days of delivery. As an authorized and supervised warehouse management company, LAFISE is responsible for quality and control of the produce in storage and in transit.

2. *Agricultural Commodities Exchange.* LAFISE has a seat on the agricultural commodity exchanges in various countries of Central America. Because these exchanges are certified by the ministries of the countries, many producers, especially cooperatives, can use them to handle domestic marketing of their products. Producers have price information to be able to sell their products for the best price, and buyers know that they are acquiring products that uphold quality standards and that have both a certificate of origin and a quality certificate.

3. *Central American payment system.* Exporters have access to the network of offices in all the countries of the region and the assurance of stable currency conversion. As a result, they enjoy great flexibility and efficiency for receiving payment on products they sell in the region.

4. *Investment fund.* LAFISE handles an investment fund of US$70 million with resources from the Inter-American Development Bank, a Norwegian investor and other European sources of financing to support small-scale businesses throughout Central America.

5. *Managed Funds.* The bank manages funds for 21 national and international organizations. Because of Nicaragua's banking regulations, it is very expensive to lend money to farmers with little collateral. Therefore, the LAFISE Group began a fund-management service for other organizations and programmes that target small-scale farmers.

6. *Commodity exchange marketing support.* Through strategic alliances with USAID, Michigan State University, Inter-American Institute for Cooperation on Agriculture, Nicaragua's Instituto de Tecnología Agropecuaria and the Commodities Exchange, LAFISE works with producers of various products to sell their crop through the agricultural commodities exchange.

7. *Loans through food processing companies.* Bancentro in Nicaragua has begun to place loans through food processing companies or consolidators, having encountered considerable difficulty trying to reach small-scale farmers directly. For example, using this value chain approach, the milk collection plant serves as an intermediary for its dairy producers granting loans for purchase of inputs and animals.

8. *Technical Assistance*. LAFISE Agropecuaria provides technical assistance directly and indirectly through facilitation of such services through NGO and governmental agencies. It directly provides technical assistance and training on specific areas such as export management and financial capacity building.

9. *Alternative financing*. Through Bancentro it provides an array of additional value chain financing services such as leasing for the purchase of equipment and machinery, asset pledging (chattel bonds or warrants), guarantee trusts, discount factoring and export finance.

10. *Insurance*. Through Seguros, LAFISE Group not only offers insurance for both the commodities that pass through the value chain, but also the range of insurance products needed by the clients and their businesses.

11. *Export*. In selected value chains, the produce is processed by Agropecuaria LAFISE and exported either within the region or to the United States.

Lessons learned

LAFISE has proven that it can be successful in working in an integrated structure throughout value chains. It has been able to grow in a relatively fast fashion from banking to multiple services. It has incorporated other value chains in step-wise fashion as it is able to ensure that it has the capacity, resources and, most importantly, a competitive market in which to operate.

A second important lesson in the LAFISE model is its acknowledgement of the value of partners. By working inclusively through partnering alliances with organizations providing technical assistance and/or other services, it has been able to incorporate many small-scale producers that otherwise would have been difficult to reach directly. In the same manner, LAFISE partners with other agribusinesses and actively works with organized producers in the Association of Exporters.

Challenges and opportunities

The most difficult challenge facing the LAFISE Group has been neither the competitive marketplace nor the lack of capacity of farmers or other difficulties within chain activities; rather it has and continues to struggle with the political uncertainty of the country, with its pressures to regulate prices, markets and/or interest rates. While value chain finance, with its linked and embedded services, is less susceptible to political manoeuvres, operating in such an environment is nevertheless much more challenging.

LAFISE is a model for consideration in other countries and regions. Few leaders have had the vision and the substantial resources to put into place the integrated model of LAFISE Group, yet through linkages and partnerships similar integrated models are possible. The model is also similar in many respects to that shown in India with the agricultural service centres, many of which are similarly initiated by a bank.

Case references

Angulo, J.E. (2007) 'Reflexiones acerca del financiamiento de cadenas agrícolas de valor', Documento de Trabajo 26, RUTA, San José, Costa Rica.
Zamora, E., (2006) presentation at the Latin American Conference.
Zamora, E. (2008) presentation at the Asia International Conference.
Website: www.lafise.com [accessed 4 October 2009].

CHAPTER 5
Innovations

Value chain finance has been rapidly evolving from its roots in relationship-based credit, to highly structured finance enabled by the integration of the chain and formalization of its processes. From basic input supplier credit provided to a known producer, to mechanisms such as warehouse receipts, the complexity and potential have grown together, as exemplified by the approaches and instruments described so far. There have been innovations in financing approaches, and technologies, and new applications of existing technologies that support chain development, and stimulate financial products and process development. Finally, there have been innovations in ways of strengthening enabling environments and support service provision. Innovation has played a critical role in the strengthening and use of value chain finance.

Value chain innovations

Advances in value chain knowledge and experience have taken place in parallel with the evolution of financial services, although the two have often developed as separate processes. In particular, an agricultural value chain is no longer viewed as a single channel that tracks a product from a farmer to a market, but as a complex chain that is impacted by relationships within the chain, enabling environments, availability of appropriate services and inputs from technology to raw materials, and most importantly, changing market demand.

Figure 5.1 illustrates the various structures and relationships that are understood to impact value chain analysis and development today. The arrows within the chain representing flows of product as well as information and services.

Value chain development practitioners and theorists have contributed significant learning regarding the basic elements of the chain, as well as the complex relationships between businesses, the viability of those businesses, the constraints and bottlenecks in the functioning of the chain, and the potential sustainable market-based solutions that can strengthen the chain's success. This means that value chain practice involves a range of next generation approaches, methods and tools such as producer group formation, association development, lobbying and advocacy, and stakeholder mediation, along with fundamental service development such as extension services, standards training, input supplies, transportation, market information, post-harvest handling and so on.

Furthermore, it is recognized that one value chain does not sit in isolation, but is part of a sub-sector – or even a global 'industry' – that is generally comprised of multiple value chains. The sub-sector might incorporate a range of products reaching different markets, crossovers between the chains,

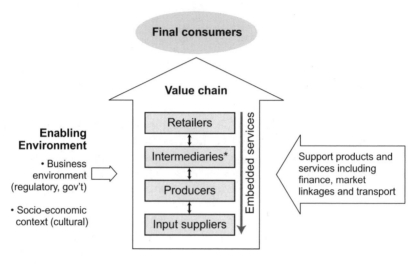

* 'Intermediaries' encompass buyers
and sellers, including processors.

Figure 5.1 A stylized value chain
Source: Miehlbradt and Jones (2007)

and activities in one channel that impact another channel. For example, the provision of processed milk to domestic urban consumers through a value chain in Bangladesh that integrates farmers, collection agents, processors, packagers and retailers, can have an impact on and be impacted by both the direct sale of raw milk to rural consumers and the distribution of imported dry milk throughout the country. This complexity of multiple chains in a sub-sector is illustrated in a simplified form in Figure 5.2 depicting an agricultural sub-sector where critical inputs that affect the various chains are

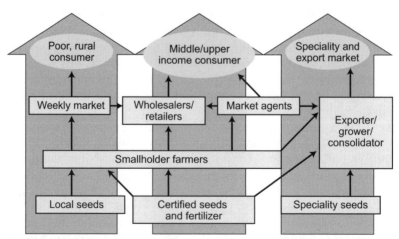

Figure 5.2 Inter-connected value chains in a sub-sector
Source: Jones (2009)

appropriate seeds and fertilizers. Innovation in value chain development is wide ranging, and many publications are available on this topic (see for example, Jones, 2009 and Harper, 2008).

It is useful, however, to distinguish between value chain structures and processes that directly encourage financing and those that do so indirectly. In the case of direct effect, a financier will examine the mechanisms and relationships to determine if the clients are creditworthy. For example, a lender will be concerned with market demand, relationships of borrowers to that market demand or to those that can access markets, strength of the specific value chain businesses, and overall functioning of the value chain. In the case of indirect influences, underlying factors that support the development of a healthy value chain are extension services, appropriate inputs, market information, producer groups, and industry associations and so on.

In summary, important value chain innovations in the agricultural sector that support the financing of the chain are:

- The development of models for market access such as contract farming, lead firm buyers, vertically integrated chains, networks of producers and buyers, and various niche markets, including organics and fair-trade.
- Assessing relationships through a range of analysis techniques: for example, value chain drivers, linkages, power relationships, and value chain control and governance.
- Development of commodity management companies with end-to-end service support options for ensuring compliance, security and quality, as well as facilitating finance.
- Commodity exchange development with rapid and accessible prices and trade opportunities for facilitating trade, risk management and opportunities for use of new financial instruments.
- The promotion of industry competitiveness through the formation of member-led industry associations, market assessment and development strategies, promotional tools, branding, product life cycle and product differentiation.

Financial innovations

Innovations in value chain finance have been largely driven by the developments in value chains themselves such as integration and formalization of relationships, the globalization of agricultural food chains, the attention from donors, facilitators and others on the role that small farmers can play in these chains, and the willingness of financiers to look at new ways to support them. Further, with the growth of microfinance, social investment, and other forms of non-conventional funding, creative forms of financing are being developed, and existing financial institutions have become more flexible and resourceful. These efforts are supported by donors who frequently offer loans or grants, guarantees, capacity building and other forms of assistance that can aid financial institutions in high risk, low collateral lending. With the deepening concerns around poverty alleviation along with the growing food crisis and the realization that even very small farmers can make an important contribution to global food security, it is anticipated that value chain development and finance will continue to change and progress. Adaptation will spur increased refinements and innovation in value chain financing, leading to new products and services that are responsive to the situation and context, and continue to mitigate risk for the lending institutions. Many of the innovations noted here are in their infancy, and continued streamlining and enhancements are expected.

The willingness of financial institutions to examine value chain relationships and make financing decisions based on third-party agreements rather than conventional collateral is one of the most significant innovations in expanding agricultural finance to poorer farmers and agro-enterprises. Whether it is an understood arrangement with a buyer like Hortifruti, a formal contract with a facilitator such as TechnoServe, or vertical integration with a global player as with Starbucks, direct lending to farmers can be improved because of these linkages. Financiers become more confident in the face of the secure markets offered by the lead firms that drive the value chain and ensure an outlet for products. Furthermore, this has led to third-party lending where banking institutions will provide loans to businesses higher in the chain – such as processors – knowing that the firm will lend to trusted suppliers. This reduces the due diligence and operational costs of lending on the part of the bank, while also mitigating their own risk.

The collateralization of agricultural outputs, and the formalization of their value, is another significant innovation in value chain finance. With the growth of managed warehouses – both low-tech field warehouses and sophisticated supply chain management establishments – lenders gain confidence in the preservation of goods, and their sustained or increased value over time. This is especially helpful to farmers and others in the chain that become able to maintain ownership beyond the high season, and sell products when markets are not glutted and prices are more favourable. This leads to higher returns and enhanced ability to repay loans and be profitable, with instruments like warehouse receipts and forward contracting being innovated as a result of this trend.

The recognition that value chain businesses, particularly smallholder farmers, have critical financing needs beyond credit has been a noteworthy development in value chain financing. The potential to offer a range of financial services is bolstered by the strength of value chains, and the spread of risk across large numbers of producers and multiple chains. Innovations in weather, crop and health insurance have helped increase their use for risk reduction, including smallholder farmers, enabling them to 'push the envelope' on productivity and cash-cropping.

Although well established as a financing approach for the 'unbankable' in general, microfinance has begun to innovate ways to become more active in

agricultural lending. Traditionally, microfinance institutions (MFIs) have focused lending on low-risk, fast-return businesses such as petty trading, but as
competition in the industry has increased, there has been greater motivation
to look at higher risk lending to farmers and agro-enterprises. MFIs have begun
to work with farmers' groups and agribusinesses in the chain to understand
their needs and risks, and then to adapt loan terms, collateral and repayment
mechanisms to match the value chain and demand. In addition to adaptation
of existing loan products, MFIs have also adopted new financing instruments,
such as leasing arrangements and financing of warehouse receipts, and savings products to help smooth incomes, accrue assets for times of need, and to
reinvest into their businesses.

Price risk reduction strategies and instruments have also undergone extensive innovations – with highly structured mechanisms such as national spot
and future exchanges. One significant innovation is the use of Internet and
cell phone applications to be able to not only share information on current
and futures prices much more broadly, even among small producers, but also
allow them to make use of that information for making forward contract sales.
This in turn allows the option to borrow funds against the sales contracts and
also to hedge risk of price reductions at the time of harvest or delivery of the
products.

Financing of supporting services to agricultural value chains – from input
and equipment suppliers to extension services and telecommunications – has
also evolved. With a firm understanding of the value chain and all its inter-
connectedness, indirect financing to the chain through support services and
products, and even partial grants, offers interesting options for value chain
growth. For example, the use of vouchers to stimulate equipment supply chains
(e.g. micro-irrigation technologies) are being trialled in Africa, and offer significant potential for increased productivity and profitability of businesses in
the chain. Innovation in financing of supporting services also extends to the
funding of suppliers who can provide non-cash disbursals of needed inputs to
farmers, repayable in-kind or cash at the time of sale. In some cases, the input
supplier and the buyer are one and the same, leading to tighter integration of
the chain and more secure repayment.

Timeliness and low transaction costs for accessing finance are critical areas
of financing to agriculture. The Kisan credit card (KCC) in India, shown in
Box 5.1 is an example of financial product innovation wherein the growers
can readily access financing from the financial system (commercial banks, rural banks and cooperative banks) and are covered both under crop insurance
and under health insurance at a nominal premium paid by the lender as loan
component.

A holistic household view of financing is creating new opportunities for
lenders and borrowers. Although there has been a greater emphasis on the
farm as a business, and the need for households to separate farm income and
expenses from family expenditures, there is also an enhanced understanding
of household income sources. In developing countries, a loan made to an

---

Box 5.1 Kisan credit cards, India

Credit products, like the Kisan (farmer) credit cards (KCC) in India, provide more accessible production, investment and consumption credit to farmers. The KCC, which has been in operation since 1998, is implemented across the country by all public sector commercial banks, regional rural banks and cooperative banks, with an outreach of over 83 million cards through March 2009 and a credit limit of US$ 8 billion. By providing both timely access to loans as well as crop and health insurance, it reduces risk of not only the producers but also their suppliers and buyers. Similar products like Grameen cards, in vogue for rural people, and Bhumiheen cards, for landless farmers/share croppers, have also been developed and introduced in the market.

Source: Balakrishnan (2007); NABARD (2009)

---

individual is frequently a loan to an extended family with diverse sources of income. So, although a loan might ostensibly be made to purchase seeds and fertilizers, repayment of that loan might come from a range of sources such as salaried or daily employment and from non-agricultural enterprise activities such as trading and small-scale manufacturing. Household income is taken into consideration in assessing the risk of lending, and offers possibilities to families that might otherwise not be considered creditworthy.

Technological innovations

New technologies and their innovative applications have supported and spurred the development of finance in general and value chain finance in particular. From the use of management information systems (MIS) to monitor stored goods in a network of warehouses, to the accessing of remittances through mobile phones, the proliferation of technology has enabled the more rapid development of affordable and accessible finance in agriculture. Enabling technologies have been well documented elsewhere, so this section focuses on the trends and specific applications that have been particularly significant to recent developments in agricultural value chain finance.

The need for technological innovations has largely been driven by issues of accessibility. Despite the global expansion of financial services, approximately two-thirds of the population in developing countries remains 'unbanked' or under-banked. Since the average cost of credit in these countries is relatively high, efficiencies stand to be gained through the application and adaptation of technological solutions, often through non-traditional and non-banking approaches such as value chains or remittances.

Management systems

Management information systems (MIS), along with other software packages and applications, are critical in managing and analysing data and generating reports relevant to value chain finance. In terms of the value chain proper, MIS have supported the development and documentation of sophisticated

---

Box 5.2 Integrated information management, BASIX, India

BASIX India is promoting the use of information management technologies in its holistic approach to development. Their initiatives and experience focus on providing a package of livelihood services that are both financial and agricultural. BASIX makes extensive use of information and communication technology in its integration of microfinance, business development and institutional development services which form part of its livelihood promotion programme. This includes value chain finance and marketing services, such as warehousing, forward contracts and insurance, as well as loans and training.

Source: Ramana (2007a)

---

processes such as traceability of agricultural products, tracking of warehouse goods, and consolidation of products for sale. With reference to finance, MIS allow portfolio and client management, structured finance instruments, commodity trading, analysis of risk, and fraud detection and control. Thus, MIS provide numerous facilities that increase access to needed information, support sound decision-making that encompasses analysis of client risk, product security, potential for trade and profitability, and so on.

A second aspect of MIS that is significant is the increasing level of sophistication of the financial and portfolio management systems of both financial and non-financial institutions to track loans, investments and cash, and in-kind accounts receivable. With sufficient 'back-office' systems of this nature, many of the value chain finance tools and processes can now be applied.

Networks and exchanges

Developments in Internet access along with reach into rural areas have enabled the creation of networks and exchanges that benefit agricultural value chains. This happens in two main ways: the delivery of critical information to farming communities such as market demand, pricing and technical advice; and the creation of exchanges that support the trade of agricultural outputs. The example from India in Box 5.3, describes an Internet application that

---

Box 5.3 Electronic network for fruit and vegetable trade, India

India is the world's second largest producer of fruits and vegetables. With the emergence of futures commodity exchanges in India and a significant increase in telecommunications and Internet access in rural India, the conditions for an electronic exchange became possible to better enable and connect large numbers of buyers and sellers. The Safal National Exchange (SNX) was developed through a joint venture between Mother Dairy Fruit and Vegetable Private Limited (MDFPL), a wholly-owned subsidiary of the National Dairy Development Board of India (NDDB), Multi-Commodity Exchange of India Ltd (MCX) and Financial Technologies India Ltd (FTIL). The exchange provides on-line price information to farmers who then plant and sell accordingly. The trading of standardized, graded produce through the exchange catalyses agribusiness activity, processing and export, due to the assurance of an uninterrupted supply of raw materials. Loans, as needed, which are linked to recovery, can be structured through banks and guaranteed with the futures contracts.

Source: Natarajan (2007)

---

serves both as an information network for farmers as well as an electronic exchange for trading of fruits and vegetables.

Mobile phones and mobile banking

Luis Corrales of the Banco Nacional de Costa Rica observed, 'We hear much talk these days about a gap between the "info-rich" and the "info-poor", this is why Costa Rica's low penetration of Internet is a critical issue.' (Corrales, 2006). Indeed, Internet, mobile phones and handheld devices have been important for the adaptation of new opportunities in value chain financing. As described in Box 5.4, India, with growing rural Internet capacity, and Kenya, with cell phones, are among those countries leading the way for such use in agriculture and agricultural finance.

In the case of implementing MIS solutions, mobile phone and handheld devices may be used at the point of data collection, and set up to transfer timely information to the larger MIS. For example, in traceability applications, field agents can track individual farmers, capture the data on a handheld device and remotely transfer the information to a central database. In turn, this central database can track availability of compliant crops and monitor expected volumes and time of market availability. In the other direction, information can be pushed out from an MIS to mobile phones and handheld devices. For example, farmers may be set up to receive alerts on changing prices for commodities and preferred market locations or buyers.

In Case 4 described at the end of this chapter, DrumNet, a project of Pride Africa in Kenya, combines mobile phones and a dedicated management information system. The MIS, developed and managed by DrumNet, captures and processes data on financing and transactions between players: farmer groups and banks, farmers and buyers, farmers and suppliers. The project works with Equity Bank and M-Pesa, a wallet service offered by Safaricom.

The fast-growing popularity of technology for use in financial transactions is evident in Kenya where the M-Pesa service has attracted 7 million registered users who are making US$2 million a day in transfers in a country where fewer

---

Box 5.4 E-choupal information centres, India

ITC introduced the concept of e-choupal, a network of IT enabled agriculture information and resource centres. Originally created for more efficient procurement of agricultural commodities in India, it has become a business platform from which a host of products and services are provided, linking the farmer to global markets, building village-level capabilities and creating economic and social value for stakeholders. Some of the real-time benefits include the enhanced decision-making power of farmers, as they know the sale price for the produce even before it leaves the village. This is done through online real-time information which bundles knowledge and information with the transactions. This knowledge is free of cost and once established in the villages or through mobile Internet kiosks is able to serve large numbers of farmers – not only with price information, but also by providing a facility to forward contract and mitigate price risks.

Source: E-choupal (2008)

than 4 million bank accounts exist (CGAP, 2009). Users can exchange cash at a retail agent in return for an electronic record of the transaction value. This virtual account is stored on the server of a non-bank service provider, such as a mobile network operator or an issuer of stored-value cards. The use of cellular devices can play a central role in both financial and value chain activities, as when mobile phones are used for remittance transfers, loan repayments, and other financial transactions with important identification data stored on the phone. This innovation goes beyond the hardware itself, and includes new kinds of relationships between banks, clients, agribusinesses and communication companies.

Point-of-sale outlets at markets or farm service centres, use of smart cards, and Internet outlets can also be used to facilitate financial transactions for input purchases and commodity sales. An example of such an application is shown in the YES Bank Agro-Food (Case Study 5) at the end of this chapter.

Infrastructural innovations

A final type of innovation for improving agricultural value chain financing is in physical infrastructure. As noted earlier, one major constraint in the use of warehouse receipt financing is the lack of suitable warehouses. Another constraint is the road, rail, river and port infrastructure. One innovative example to address the logistical constraints in the Philippines is described in Box 5.5.

Box 5.5 Transportation innovation in the Philippines

A flagship programme of the Development Bank of the Philippines (DBP), the Sustainable Logistics Development Program (SLDP), that addresses the logistical needs of the distribution of goods and services within the context of the government's goals of global competitiveness, poverty alleviation and food sufficiency at the local, regional, and national levels. The financial assistance of SLDP focuses on the physical asset requirements of a sustainable distribution system of maritime transport and related land transport. It is geared towards the development of progressive long-haul shipping to constitute the country's national backbone in the transport of bulk agricultural products and the development of a short-haul ferry system to link the islands to the growth centres of the country. One component of the SLDP is a terminal system for farmers and traders called the roll-on-roll-off terminal system (RRTS). The roll-on–roll-off terminals and ferry operations will be established in areas where such services are absent or are only serviced by small wooden boats. The RRTS form part of the national highways providing the necessary linkage and efficiency to inter-island travel and transport. The concept is effective in archipelagos like the Philippines because it uses the vessels to function as bridges in connecting roads on both sides of the seas. With the RRTS in place in strategic regions of the archipelago, fast and efficient movement of goods can enable farmers and traders to simply roll-on their vehicles to these 'floating bridges', and roll-off from the vessels to their respective destinations. This can not only spur growth in rural areas, but also reduce migration to urban centres. Working capital needs of small farmers, traders and entrepreneurs are also assisted through DBP's micro and small enterprise lending programmes. Larger investments in capital equipment and fixed assets, including ferries and bulk carriers, reefers, silos and other cargo handling and storage equipment, are supported by DBP's project financing programmes such as the SLDP.

Source: Lazaro (2007)

The RRTS system is a major investment to address a critical bottleneck in chain development. Infrastructural development of roads, storage, ports and other requirements are often serious constraints to value chain development which are left unaddressed in large part because of the significant investment costs and the slow, long-term returns on capital. In order to facilitate this infrastructural financing, value chain financing through instruments such as forfaiting, which are relatively innovative in the agricultural sector, can be considered.

Policy and public sector innovations

Policy and public sector innovations for value chain financing are often subtle and indirect. In fact in some cases, improvements have been made from simply having less governmental intervention – less subsidy or price controls, for example, that stifle strong value chain development. Public support to producer groups, market development programmes or even research will not be effective if not linked to value chains. Innovative public interventions focus on demand and addressing the areas of weakness in the vertical and horizontal linkages within agricultural chains, giving priority to those which are most strategic in terms of the economy and the social outcomes (see Box 5.6).

Agri-export zones (AEZs) in India are another example of public policy innovations that promote value chains for agricultural export products. AEZs were identified based on the availability of a particular agriculture product in a region and the potential for further development of the entire value chain.

As noted by banking and agribusiness experts in India, innovation holds the key for boosting growth in the agriculture sector. This is a major undertaking and is illustrated in Box 5.7. Innovations are often a result of public and private cooperation, with policy support, which opens the doors for profitable businesses in stronger and more secure value chains and consequently more

---

Box 5.6 Value chain approach to agricultural services, Costa Rica

In 2006, the Ministry of Agriculture changed its programming and extensive services toward a value chain approach. In a major structural shift, the Ministry undertook assessment of all the value chains within each district. After selecting priority value chains for intervention based on the importance and the level of need for improvement in the particular chains, coordinators were assigned at the national and district levels and extension work changed from a multi-faceted approach to a chain focused one. Also important to the process was an effort to significantly increase the involvement of private sector agribusinesses as well as governmental and non-governmental organizations involved with those value chains. Financing, through financial institutions, and public investment in both physical infrastructure and capacity development is directed towards identified needs. An evaluation of the process showed progress and continued interest in the approach.

Source: Díaz (2008)

Box 5.7 Agri-export zones in India

The Government of India has identified 60 product-specific agri-export zones (AEZs) for chain development. The effort is centred on a cluster approach with support activities, infrastructure and services required for development of these export-oriented value chains in the respective geographical regions in which these products are grown. The governmental support includes special financing packages for contract farming and fiscal incentives for infrastructural development and support services, including financial institutions which service the entire value chain with specially designed financial products and services.

An example of an AEZ can be seen in the onion sector of Maharashtra State which lacked storage and financing to improve value addition. With an investment of US$85 million under a 60-40 per cent partnership investment with the private sector, the government extended training to 5,500 farmers on production and post-harvest management for continuous flow of product, post-harvest facility and other infrastructural development and export facilitation for agro-industries leading to the export of 55,000 metric tonnes within two years.

Source: Das and Baria (2005)

---

access to financing. Key areas of innovation which need such support to be incubated and replicated were noted as:

- Enhancement and replication of Information and Communication Technology (ICT).
- Improved risk management tools (crop and weather risk insurance, futures and options).
- Enhanced service provision (integration of service facilitator companies into value chains).
- Group aggregation (farmers' associations and self-help group links).
- Expansion of financing models (contractual farming, warehouse receipts, collateral management, leasing, equity finance, supply and structured commodity finance).
- Greater use and inclusion of national spot and futures exchanges. (Ghore, 2007)

Introduction to the Case Studies

The following two case studies are examples of moving beyond the conventional models of finance and value chain development.

In the DrumNet Case Study from Kenya, technology is applied to the value chain finance model to facilitate the reduction of costs and improve efficiency in reaching small farmers. The result is their integration into commercial value chains and sources of finance.

The subsequent Case Study, from India, describes how agro-food parks are being developed to leverage economies of scale and improve efficiency. This offers small producers and businesses the opportunity to be competitive in commercial markets while enabling commercial banks to reach new markets for financial and agribusiness services.

Case Study 4. DrumNet and technological innovations

Jonathan Campaigne, Founder, DrumNet and Pride Africa

Background

Agriculture represents the largest economic sector in most African countries and remains the greatest opportunity for economic growth and poverty alleviation, both at a national and a household level. Research continues to reinforce conventional wisdom and grassroots opinion that it is financial and market constraints that inhibit sector growth, particularly among rural smallholder farmers, most living at or below the poverty line. In Kenya, these constraints are particularly frustrating because the key players required for a vibrant smallholder agricultural sector are present – commercial banks, large-scale produce buyers, farm input suppliers, transporters, and the smallholders themselves. One critical factor inhibiting development is a networking platform for intermediation of the flow of information and financial transactions among partners engaged in the production, financing, and marketing of agricultural produce.

Bank and microfinance institution financing of farm inputs and crops have experienced poor repayment rates, and high transaction costs. Exporters have ventured into smallholder group extension activity and out-grower credit schemes with mixed results to ensure reliable supplies of produce for their core business of export marketing. Rural, mostly independent, small-scale input suppliers often sell their seeds and agro-chemicals on credit to increase farmer demand, but in the process reduce their ability to maintain stocks or generate profits. Finally, smallholder self-help groups and cooperatives – powerful organizations for information sharing and aggregation of produce – have proven to be unreliable vehicles for basic financial services such as credit provision, payment distribution, or savings mobilization. Thus, while there is a demand for networking services between those in the value chain, it is clear that only an independent cross-cutting organization, focused on this niche as the core business, can successfully deliver those services required to truly break through the constraints that cripple the sector's development.

The organization targeting this opportunity would need to structure itself largely as an information network, based on a standardized set of rules and processes, tracking large volumes of data and triggering disparate financial transactions, and acting as a secure gateway of data and funds for participants in the agricultural sector. In abstract, the concept parallels existing virtual networks such as Visa or ATM (Automated Teller Machine) networks, e-commerce exchanges such as eBay, or even equity or commodity exchanges – financial intermediation platforms for structuring and executing various types of common business transactions. These highly successful organizations have developed and maintained a set of policies and rules, embodied in networked information technology systems that are generally sustained through retained transaction fees or commissions. However, creating such a network in rural communities for smallholder farmers with minimal infrastructure support is particularly challenging without a physical presence, thus eliminating the possibility of a completely virtual network. However, through involvement of rural organizations the chance for such a network remains a viable and eventually a sustainable opportunity.

DrumNet

DrumNet, a pilot project of PRIDE AFRICA, was launched in March 2003 as a new rural value chain management system targeted at smallholder farmers in Kenya. The vision of DrumNet is a management system linking value chain partners through DrumNet policies, processes and IT systems. The DrumNet system facilitates a set of financial, marketing, and information transactions which are designed to directly impact the productivity of small-scale farmers and indirectly, related stakeholders in Africa. DrumNet is currently donor sponsored, and is developing a commercial model that will lead to an independent, self funding and sustainable African organization.

Financing farmers

In urban areas worldwide, microfinance has shown its potency to reach the poor, and prove that the poor are bankable; however PRIDE AFRICA was not alone in realizing that serving poor, rural farmers, who comprise over 75 per cent of the continent's population, required a different approach. The combination of higher operating costs in rural areas to serve a dispersed customer base, infrequent sales revenues due to long planting and harvesting cycles, and low profit margins, had excluded conventional microfinance as a solution to low rural productivity and incomes. Without subsidies, rural finance has proven to be commercially unsustainable.

Initially, DrumNet's concept was to directly link key players along the agricultural value chain – commercial banks, smallholder farmers, and retail providers of farm inputs – through a cashless credit programme and integrated marketing and payments system. This objective was revised and extended at an early stage of the project to focus more specifically on increasing smallholder incomes. To this end the value chain was extended to include buyers of agricultural produce and to place them at the centre of the chain.

DrumNet does not rely on high margins and fast turnover of inventory that underpins conventional microfinance; instead, the model depends on contracts, technology, management systems, and structured finance. The DrumNet design and approach is to link major commercial agro-processors, agribusiness investors and buyers to groups of poor farmers via purchase contracts and master contract frameworks that include all the members of the farm-to-buyer value chain, input suppliers, and commercial banks. The power of purchase contracts to drive the value chain model cannot be overstated. With a contract in hand, and DrumNet supplying the contractual framework and standards, farmers' groups could produce and sell and avoid market risk.

DrumNet partners with other organizations to provide capacity building in farmer group dynamics, training and certification to assure the buyer of the quality required. As the buyer specifies the quantity, quality and price upfront, the farmer then has the means to buy the right kind of inputs on affordable credit terms necessary to fulfil the contract. The contractual framework is the backbone of the DrumNet model. Not only do purchase contracts formalize the sell–buy linkage, but they have credit value at banks due to the high credit standing of the buyer.

On the finance side of the model, DrumNet stepped back from the traditional microfinance approach of being a supplier of credit, and concentrated on working with a commercial bank to structure credit and banking services to producer groups based on the sales proceeds paid by the buyer that flow through the bank. A value chain management system is a recognized financing model that connects members of a production pipeline as if they were departments within a single company. Supporting DrumNet's connectivity between its members is an information communication technology (ICT) platform integrating technical, telecommunication, information management, and credit structuring. The DrumNet ICT platform maps all the members, logistics, credit flows, payments, and accounting events into an agricultural value chain management system. In the absence of the ICT, DrumNet could not exist and would not have existed five years ago because of the inefficiencies of paper based data collection, accounting, and dispute resolution.

The DrumNet customers

DrumNet's target clients are farmers in Kenya with land holdings of up to two acres, typically growing a mixture of subsistence and cash crops. These farmers live at or slightly below the poverty line. They are unable to access formal marketing channels on an equitable basis and typically are out of reach of commercial banks and MFIs (the latter largely focusing on urban/peri-urban non-farm microenterprises). DrumNet also targets female farmers who are more vulnerable to poverty in Kenya. Sixty nine per cent of economically active females work as subsistence farmers, compared to 43 per cent of men.

The business model

The business model is straight forward. DrumNet unites producers, large agro-buyers, suppliers and commercial banks into an efficient end-to-end finance, production, delivery and payment process. DrumNet facilitates and brokers services to a value chain where certified farm groups stand on the producing/ selling side, a reputable buyer on the buying side, and certified input suppliers and a commercial bank in the middle. A large and reputable agro-processing company, the 'buyer', signs a fixed price purchase contract with the farmer groups under a master contract managed by DrumNet. The DrumNet master contract represents the roles, rights and obligations of all parties in the value

The model creates efficiencies and allows participants to enter markets or improve access to partners.

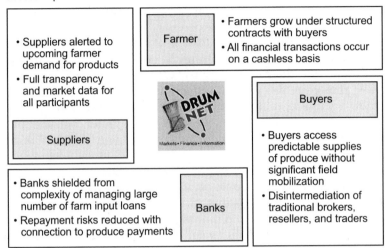

Figure 5.3 The DrumNet actors
Source: case author, Campaigne

chain. Subcontracts between parties define the obligations of each specific actor. The contract's sales proceeds flow through the bank to repay all production credit and fees owed by the producer.

DrumNet's ICT system provides the internal controls to monitor transactions and contract compliance and to report on all the movements of factors and funds within the value chain. For its brokerage, administrative and transactional services, DrumNet charges fee shares from its value chain partners and members.

The value chain model works on the basis of a series of contracts between DrumNet and the four key players along the value chain, namely producers, buyers, input suppliers/stockists and banks. The contracts involving buyers and producers are at the centre of the proposition. In summary, the roles and responsibilities of the stakeholders are as follows:

Farmers. They must belong to existing registered self-help groups as they must be a legal entity to enter into a contract. Each farmer group nominates one of their members as Transaction Agent (TA) to represent them in transactions. These agents operate rural collection points, receiving produce from member farmers and facilitating grading, packing and issuance of receipts by the buyer's agent. Depending on the crop and the value chain actor requirements, the system will be able to cater for individual farmers as well. Transaction agents also provide basic information to member farmers. For these part-time services, the TA is paid a small commission. Beyond this, under the contract, the TA is responsible for all DrumNet communication, production and banking activities by his/her group.

A group is contracted to grow and produce the variety of the crop required by the buyer and to follow agronomic practices as set down by the buyer to achieve quality. Farmers may take production loans in-kind in the form of inputs, provided they can supply the necessary security required by banks and repay the loans through crop sales. Individual farmers who do not meet their contractual obligations are ejected from the group. Each group must open a bank account with the participating bank through which all payments can be made, thus creating a cashless system. Each member is required to contribute to a transaction insurance fund (TIF) of 25 per cent of the value of loans, which acts as a security for the loan, demonstrates commitment, and begins the process of members understanding and complying with DrumNet regulations.

DrumNet outsources the farmer group training and certification to a competent partner to impart the farming management skills required to effectively use the seeds and input package that the buyer dictates in the contract. A critical purpose of the training and certification is to reduce the buyer's risk of inferior seed quality and diminished value due to poor management methods.

At the end of the production cycle – about 5 months in the case of sunflower seeds – the farmer groups deliver their produce at pre-identified collection centres. The buyer verifies acceptable quality and authorizes immediate payment, paying the farmer group through the bank, which sets up a single purpose DrumNet cash management account to receive sales proceeds and subtract repayment of outstanding principal and interest, DrumNet fees and any other obligations specified in the DrumNet/farmer group contract. After servicing all authorized obligations, the bank transfers the net balance in the cash management account to the account of the farmers' group.

The producer value proposition is higher income and liquidity than the farmer could otherwise earn due to a contract with a reliable market/buyer and a source of finance to take advantage of the market opportunity. The group organization is essential to keep transaction costs manageable.

Buyer. The buyer is the pivotal actor in the network, providing the market opportunities and contracts with farmers for production, harvest and the means of transportation and delivery of produce. The buyer:

- Contracts the amounts of seed to be planted and volumes to be harvested, quality and grading standards, the prices to be paid and expected delivery schedules, all in advance of the planting season.
- Coordinates transportation of produce from identified and agreed upon collection centres.
- Provides extension services through use of DrumNet certified trainers to the participating farmer groups to ensure that the recommended inputs are utilized and correct farming methodologies are used.
- Pays 80 per cent of the agreed price to the farmers, with the balance on receipt at the buyers' premises following quality control checks. Title to the crop changes hands on delivery.

The value proposition for buyers is predictable quantities, qualities and delivery times due to access to trained and reliable farmers, a dedicated value chain management system and quality control systems.

Input suppliers/stockists. DrumNet certified suppliers and stockists deliver a buyer-defined package of seeds and inputs to eligible farm groups in accordance with the requirements set down by the buyers in the master DrumNet contract provisions. DrumNet farmer groups pay for their inputs through the bank on a cashless basis when a line of credit is in place. The bank's payment to the supplier is charged to the farmer group line of credit. Liquidity (immediate payment) is a large incentive to a stockist. In certain cases, farmer groups may pay the supplier in cash when the input purchases are small.

The value proposition for input suppliers is increased sales. Input suppliers are no longer required to take the credit risk for supply of inputs to smallholder farmers and can increase their local market share as a trusted link in the network.

Banks. Banks provide loans to farmers for the purchase of inputs and provide transactional banking services. They pay stockists for inputs, recover loans and interest from buyer payments, and credit farmer accounts with the surpluses. Banks can also offer additional financial products and services to farmer group members but these lie outside the DrumNet network.

The value proposition for banks is net interest income, fee revenue, and an expanded deposit base. The whole value chain model and cash management system mitigates the banks' credit risk. Access to a virtually untapped wholesale client base also provides cost-effective risk diversification.

Key DrumNet features

- Inputs are available to farmer groups under contract to the buyer.
- Credit limits are based on production capability determined by DrumNet analysis.
- The farmer groups' source of loan repayment is sales proceeds on the buyer self-liquidating produce purchase contract.
- Repayment is collected at source from sales proceeds directed by the buyer into special DrumNet cash management account (Lockbox) at the bank for concentration of funds and controlled disbursement. The bank will have first claim on the sales proceeds flowing through Lockbox.
- Credit risk management is based on a combination of purchase order quality (the buyer), and cash collateral placed by farmer groups equal to 25 per cent of credit advances, which will be in a DrumNet blocked account (TIF) in the bank.
- The software is designed in such a fashion that it can be configured to address each licensee's particular needs either from the buyer perspective, the agro-dealers' requirements including both input and output channels, the farmer group, the transporters or the bank, or from an investor or donor vantage point.

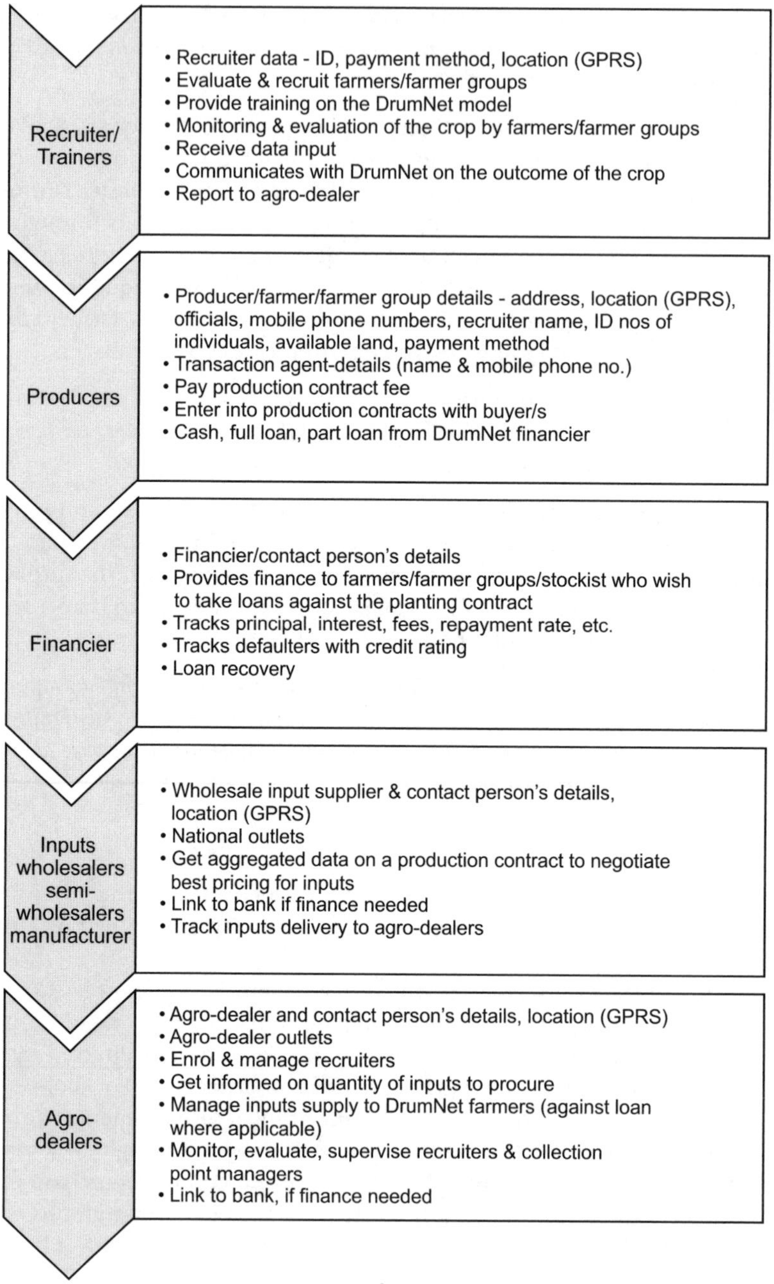

Recruiter/ Trainers	• Recruiter data - ID, payment method, location (GPRS) • Evaluate & recruit farmers/farmer groups • Provide training on the DrumNet model • Monitoring & evaluation of the crop by farmers/farmer groups • Receive data input • Communicates with DrumNet on the outcome of the crop • Report to agro-dealer
Producers	• Producer/farmer/farmer group details - address, location (GPRS), officials, mobile phone numbers, recruiter name, ID nos of individuals, available land, payment method • Transaction agent-details (name & mobile phone no.) • Pay production contract fee • Enter into production contracts with buyer/s • Cash, full loan, part loan from DrumNet financier
Financier	• Financier/contact person's details • Provides finance to farmers/farmer groups/stockist who wish to take loans against the planting contract • Tracks principal, interest, fees, repayment rate, etc. • Tracks defaulters with credit rating • Loan recovery
Inputs wholesalers semi-wholesalers manufacturer	• Wholesale input supplier & contact person's details, location (GPRS) • National outlets • Get aggregated data on a production contract to negotiate best pricing for inputs • Link to bank if finance needed • Track inputs delivery to agro-dealers
Agro-dealers	• Agro-dealer and contact person's details, location (GPRS) • Agro-dealer outlets • Enrol & manage recruiters • Get informed on quantity of inputs to procure • Manage inputs supply to DrumNet farmers (against loan where applicable) • Monitor, evaluate, supervise recruiters & collection point managers • Link to bank, if finance needed

Figure 5.4a Process flow
Source: case author, Campaigne

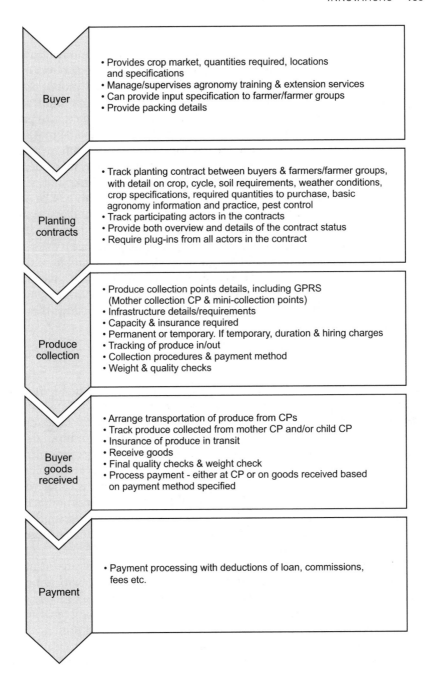

Buyer
- Provides crop market, quantities required, locations and specifications
- Manage/supervises agronomy training & extension services
- Can provide input specification to farmer/farmer groups
- Provide packing details

Planting contracts
- Track planting contract between buyers & farmers/farmer groups, with detail on crop, cycle, soil requirements, weather conditions, crop specifications, required quantities to purchase, basic agronomy information and practice, pest control
- Track participating actors in the contracts
- Provide both overview and details of the contract status
- Require plug-ins from all actors in the contract

Produce collection
- Produce collection points details, including GPRS (Mother collection CP & mini-collection points)
- Infrastructure details/requirements
- Capacity & insurance required
- Permanent or temporary. If temporary, duration & hiring charges
- Tracking of produce in/out
- Collection procedures & payment method
- Weight & quality checks

Buyer goods received
- Arrange transportation of produce from CPs
- Track produce collected from mother CP and/or child CP
- Insurance of produce in transit
- Receive goods
- Final quality checks & weight check
- Process payment - either at CP or on goods received based on payment method specified

Payment
- Payment processing with deductions of loan, commissions, fees etc.

Figure 5.4b Process flow
Source: case author, Campaigne

Technology

During phase one, PRIDE AFRICA designed a simple model and database to cater for the limited transactions and serve as a basis for scaling-up to a more robust replicable model. Work was done with farmer groups and mobile phone transactions. A more focused and specialized database and communication structure is now under development that will standardize and digitize information along the material and financial value chain. The goal is that each farmer group can be linked to the other actors in the value chain in a rapid and economical manner. The platform will be designed and implemented as an integrated, automated system to provide interactive links and reconciliation between all actors in the agricultural value chain. This will be done through mobile phones to Internet transmission. A database and MIS system will capture and process the data integrating financial and transactional exchanges between the actors using a general packet radio service (GPRS) network which is an 'always on', and private network for data to and from GPRS mobile devices. The DrumNet value chain management system will reconcile, analyse, and report the chain of input delivery events, credit draw downs, product delivery events, invoices, payments and other financial flows through the system.

Financial arrangements

The bank extends lines of credit to the farm groups for production purposes. A line of credit provides short-term loan advances to farmer groups to purchase seeds, fertilizers and other inputs stipulated under the DrumNet/buyer contract. Under the line of credit, the amount of short-term advances are determined by the input value needed to satisfy specific purchase order contracts from the buyer to the group. Inputs are supplied under contract to the farmer groups from certified suppliers. Repayment of the credit line is collected directly from the sales proceeds the buyer pays into the dedicated DrumNet cash management account ('DrumNet Lockbox'). In this structured arrangement, DrumNet steps out from the direct lending role that PRIDE AFRICA performed in its microfinance network.

The bank is a motivated partner. DrumNet brings an aggregate 'relationship' group to the bank: the members of the value chain. The bank not only achieves profitability targets and reduces credit risk, but increases its deposit base which under banking regulations enlarges the bank's lending capacity. In addition, working with the bank, DrumNet is co-creating and testing a new banking product to serve rural commodity producers – a credit default risk management facility as a reinsurance fund for the bank to cover bank losses in excess of the TIF. Although the likelihood of usage is low, its role is to comfort banks until they gain full confidence in the chain participants.

The project development phases

Phase I: Pilot (2004–2006). DrumNet's platform prototype was built during a pilot project in central Kenya involving approximately 1,250 farmers growing high value horticultural crops for export. Phase one, with funding from the International Development Research Centre (IDRC), IFAD and Monsanto, saw the completion of the research and development to build the basic model, and create and test the ICT platform. PRIDE AFRICA created a simple model and database to cater for limited transactions and serve as a basis for scaling-up a more robust, replicable model. The review of the pilot project determined that it had a positive impact on smallholder farmers, although individual farmer transaction costs were too high. Further conclusions drawn from the pilot phase include:

- *Buyer-driven linkages.* It is important that linkages be driven by the demand from buyers of agricultural produce. They must be supplied with the produce they require in terms of quality, quantity, timing, packaging, etc.
- *Insufficient collateral for banks.* The security afforded by the TIF, group guarantees and the presence of buyer contracts proved inadequate during phase one, which drew heavily on the DrumNet guarantee facility. This implies the continued need for a partial guarantee facility, at least until farmers build up a sufficient credit history. Moreover, the pilot did not fully test the ability of banks to design a loan product that meets the needs of seasonal agriculture.
- *Process and institutional linkages.* It is important to involve major input suppliers in the network to ensure agro-input stockists have the correct products available at the right time, and to improve product grading, quality control and delivery processes and responsibilities between buyers and farmers, to avoid problems of supply and quality.

Phase II: Commercial viability (2007–2010). A second project phase was introduced in August 2007 to continue work on DrumNet and investigate if its platform could be scaled to a level that might prove commercially viable given DrumNet's operational approach. Phase two was launched in western Kenya, in cooperation with BIDCO, Equity Bank, and Farmer Field Schools (FFS) – a nationally organized network of farmer groups originally established by FAO

Table 5.1 Performance indicators

	September 2007	March 2008	September 2008
No. of farmers	288	275	1,365
Acres pledged	187	155	1,300
Projected kgs	140,250	116,250	975,000
Delivered kgs	11,818	11,209	61,876

Source: case author, Campaigne

with assistance from the Gates Foundation. DrumNet has since expanded from Nyanza province to Nakuru and Embu, leading to substantial expansion between the March 2008 and September 2008 growing seasons.

Phase two is the proof of concept stage, testing the commerciality of the financial value chain management system. The project plan envisages fast growth in the number of smallholders involved in the future. Consequently, the team is working to refine and complete the DrumNet communications and payments system. Concurrently, they are working with new prospective partners to negotiate and conclude contracts in other commodities which will significantly increase the financial and social impact and move the stage of development from start-up to take-off.

Phase III: DrumNet high growth. Rapid expansion of farmer participation is projected by ramping up the number of buyers of agricultural commodities, the number of banks providing a standardized value chain model structured financial product, and the number of producer groups into more markets and countries. More transactions provide a greater degree of sustainability and profitability. Also, by phase three, PRIDE AFRICA intends that the ICT platform will be able to standardize and digitize information that will allow a greater level of tracking with reconciliation down to the individual farmer unit. PRIDE AFRICA has begun the business planning process to commercialize the DrumNet value chain management system. The scalability of the approach will be a direct result of achieving the growth and financial margin outcomes in phase two.

The working objectives during the three phases are: 1) Achieve operational self sufficiency in three years; 2) Grow to become a commercially viable business in five years, reaching 500,000–1,000,000 clients throughout eastern and southern Africa; and 3) Demonstrate that the DrumNet value chain management system is a commercially viable proposition that can be widely replicated.

Sustainability strategy

The most powerful drivers of its commercial sustainability will be profit margins and growth. With the ICT proven effective in phase two, DrumNet will be capable of digitally processing a significant volume of transactions. To achieve financial break even, it needs revenues to cover operations and fund asset growth. DrumNet can generate revenue from license fees, membership fees, transaction fees, credit spreads (shared with the bank), credit enhancement guarantee fees, and brokerage fees. DrumNet's aim is to charge a service fee on every transaction facilitated by the system to enable it to share in the incremental value gained by the members. These fees are modest and competitive as compared to agro-brokerage operations.

DrumNet, as a technology company has high operating leverage which means that most of its costs are fixed expenses because DrumNet transactions are performed digitally through the ICT platform. Hence, volume is essential for profitability. PRIDE AFRICA plans to grow the DrumNet network aggressively, linking smallholder farmers to commercial financial service providers, farm input suppliers, and agricultural buyers throughout Kenya, East Africa and eventually the entire continent. To meet these requirements, its growth must be cost effective, replicable and scalable. As such, PRIDE AFRICA is designing its business with a clear eye towards standards and partnerships. To facilitate the rapid expansion, DrumNet will offer its services through a variety of channels. During the business model testing phase, DrumNet is operating small business support centres that are embedded with other existing organizations. Initially in Central and Western provinces DrumNet focused on farmer groups through DrumNet field offices which proved too expensive to replicate. The model is being enhanced to leverage agro-dealers who offer a promising business network for the input and output markets. International agencies, private sector businesses and investors have shown interest in the model as a unique tool to link farmers and buyers. By developing standardized service packages and operational processes, these centres can be operated within existing co-operatives, banks, SACCOs, MFIs and other institutions. Similar to a franchise model, these embedded centres will 'plug' into the growing DrumNet network and will enjoy the advantages of a large, growing network of data, customers, partners, and shared resources.

Currently sponsored by international donor agencies, the vision for DrumNet is a wide-spread, distributed network of partners, sharing and improving the DrumNet platform. The goal is facilitating financial, marketing, and information transactions which directly stimulate wealth creation and economic integration of small-scale farmers, particularly women, in Africa.

Case Study 5. Integrated agro food parks: avenues for sustainable agricultural development in India

Kalyan Chakravathy, Advisor, YES Bank, and Raju Poosapati, Sr. Vice-President and Head Food & Agribusiness, YES Bank.

Summary

This case study identifies critical issues hampering Indian agriculture and presents key imperatives to strengthen agricultural value chains in India. It showcases knowledge-based banking and integrated financial value chain solutions to realize higher growth trajectory for sustainable agricultural development, while effectively addressing major deterrents and the prospects presented by Integrated Agro Food Parks (IAFPs).

Overview: the need for innovation

India's GDP recently crossed the trillion-dollar mark making it a member of the elite club of the twelve countries with 'trillion dollar economies'. Accounting for 18.3 per cent of the nation's GDP, the agriculture sector has been the means of livelihood for almost two-thirds of its work force. Though the sector's contribution to GDP has been declining over the years, the Indian economy is still influenced to a great extent by agricultural production, reflected predominantly by the strong correlation between change in agricultural GDP and overall GDP. It can therefore, be safely deduced that the growth trajectory for the economy could have been far better if the agricultural sector performed more strongly.

The primary reason behind the alienation of the agriculture sector in India's growth story has been the stagnation or fall of investment in agriculture since the mid-1990s and the resultant decline of the share of the agricultural sector's capital formation in the country's GDP. The higher transaction costs associated with dispersed populations and inadequate infrastructure, along with the particular needs and higher risk factors inherent to agriculture have resulted in an under provision of financial services in rural areas, and if available, products that are often designed without any consideration for the needs and capacities of rural households and agricultural producers.

Irrespective of the deficiencies encountered across the agri-value chain such as low productivity due to paltry investment and lack of technical know-how, and critical value chain inefficiencies such as poor logistics, multiplicity of intermediaries, inadequate marketing infrastructure, lack of focus on quality standards and minimal processing leading to post harvest losses of US$ 11 billion, India could meet its demand for agricultural produce, mostly by indigenous production. However, buoyant and rapidly increasing demand of agricultural produce calls for immediate measures to streamline the agri-value chains while plugging value seepage at various levels.

About YES BANK

YES BANK Ltd., a customer service driven, private Indian bank catering to 'emerging India', has 117 branches, and offers customized and comprehensive banking and financial solutions to its customers, including corporate and institutional banking, financial markets, investment banking, business and transactional banking, retail banking and private banking.

One of the key strengths and differentiating features of YES BANK is its knowledge-driven approach to banking for food and agribusiness as well as other selected sectors which is the essence of all offerings to its customers. The knowledgeable bankers offer invaluable and in-depth insights into their sectors of expertise, thereby helping clients to develop their business plans and activities, and nurture them to fruition by sharing business ideas and creating customized solutions for clients' specific requirements.

As a bank committed to rural India, it has set up the Food and Agribusiness Strategic Advisory and Research (FASAR) division by mobilizing a team of experienced industry and banking professionals who have the necessary knowledge and skills sets in identified sectors. These food and agribusiness experts work with the stakeholders in the food chain in various capacities to develop risk mitigating and innovative project structures for enhanced financing of the sector. This results in increased commercial viability and ensures sustainable development of agricultural value chains.

The fact that agriculture lending constitutes a major 23.91 per cent of the total portfolio of US$1,924.65 million, as against a minimum of 18 per cent of net bank credit (NBC) stipulated by the Reserve Bank of India, explains the strong commitment to develop this sector. The percentage share of agriculture in the portfolio, that specifically directs lending to the farm sector, has been increasing steadily since 2006–07. Agriculture lending has increased from US$295.32 million in 2006–07 to US$460.16 million in 2008–09, with US$351.69 million of direct agriculture lending and a balance of US$108.47 million of indirect agriculture lending, against US$183.51 million of direct agriculture and US$111.81 million of indirect agriculture lending in 2006–07. Further, the non-performing assets of the advances to the agricultural sector by YES BANK are less than 0.01 per cent when compared to 3.18 per cent national average of all banks, and reinforces the strong focus and robustness of product offering.

The value chain forms an integral part of decision-making for any organization as the entire production of its goods and services depends on its efficiency and effectiveness. The YES BANK's knowledge approach analyses the value chain, works with and understands the stakeholders and their transactions and applies integrated financial value chain solutions to meet their financial needs. These customized products and services include letters of credit, advances, warehouse receipt finance, bill collection, pre-finance, post-shipment finance, factoring and guarantees. Examples wherein these products were deployed to address specific needs of its customers occurred when Yes Bank provided:

- Structured finance to about 2,000 nomadic honey farmers from Northern India, in partnership with one of the largest exporters of honey from India, see Box 5.8.
- Trade finance for the traditional craftsmen associated with a Mumbai-based NGO for exhibiting their artifacts in 'gateway to India' exhibition in New York.
- Finance to sugarcane farmers associated with various sugar mills.
- Finance to small and marginal farmers for purchasing drip-irrigation systems under a Central Government Sponsored Micro-Irrigation Project (CGSMIP).

Box 5.8 Warehousing of nomadic farmers' honey in northern India

Honey producers are now able to deposit their honey in warehouses managed by the YES Bank appointed collateral manager who assesses its quality and quantity. The honey is pledged as security without transfer of title or possession. The honey receipts are used for borrowing from the bank, which will lend up to 70 per cent of the price of the honey offered from a large honey exporter, Kashmir Apiaries Export (KAE), with whom YES Bank has set an agreement. However, the beekeepers are free to sell to whichever buyer is the highest bidder at the time he/she decides to sell. By not having to sell at harvest, and being able to achieve prices averaging 50 per cent higher and loans rates much lower, total volume of sales of KAE has more than doubled to over US$17 million.

Source: case authors, Chakravathy and Poosapati

Integrated value chain development model

YES BANK believes that a knowledge-based project development approach is needed to transform Indian agriculture thus benefiting all stakeholders including farmers, companies, government and overall the Indian society. The key is to structure and finance bankable agribusiness projects for broad-based development of the agricultural sector, leading to economically and ecologically sustainable development.

Given the inter-linkages between the independent value chain components across the agri-value chain (see Figure 5.5) there is a need for an integrated and

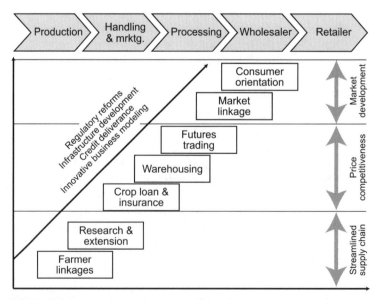

Figure 5.5 A holistic perspective: agricultural value chain approach
Source: case authors, Poosapati and Chakravathy

holistic approach, involving *'value creators'* and *'enablers'* bringing in regulatory reforms, infrastructure development, credit and other financial services
and innovative business structuring to maximize stakeholders benefits, to
farmers and consumers in particular, and to achieve overall development of
the sector.

Value addition, through rural service centres, offers one solution. Such centres, although relatively new in India, have been developed under various
schemes using a basic model of integrated services such as agricultural inputs,
finance, technical advice, warehousing, and marketing. Models include the
Kisan-Bandu which uses village business centres, e-Choupal employing electronic services, along with agricultural service and *Hariyali Kisaan* Bazaars aim-
ing to provide all encompassing services under one roof.

The YES BANK model uses rural transformation centres (RTCs) linked to
Integrated Agricultural Food Parks (IAFP). This model provides a platform for
spatial clustering of varied agro- production chains while effectively addressing the inherent deficiencies of the corresponding system. An IAFP, with modern production and processing facilities is linked to the RTCs located in the
catchments as *integral supply linkages* integrating farmers with the demand side
of the food chain in an efficient manner. Technical know-how on management practices are shared with the farmers linked to the IAFP as well as state-
of-the-art processing technologies made available at the park. This enhances
the quality and productivity and thereby renders increased acceptability and
competitiveness of Indian foods in international markets (see Figure 5.6). The
IAFPs also act as a linkage for agri-biotechnology companies, fruits and vegetables, grain/oil seed trading and processing companies, meat production and
processing companies and farmers/producers by working together to educate
the professionals of the future and develop food science and technology at
large.

An IAFP offers a robust framework for value chain finance by way of providing access to credit in terms of customized products, specific to the needs of
various stakeholders at different levels of the agri-value chain, thus facilitating adequate investment crucial for higher returns. The same is illustrated in
Figure 5.7 using oil processing value chain in the IAFP context.

The IAFP ensures higher returns to various stakeholders due to enhanced
productivity, better traceability, higher quality output and off-season availability. The interdependent linkages of the agri-value chain and the security
of a market-driven demand for the final product provides the producers and
processors with an assured market for their products thereby addressing issues
like distress sale which has been the major trigger for default and credit risk. It
makes it easier for various stakeholders, especially farmers, to obtain finance at
a lower cost from banks. This model helps YES BANK in financial inclusion of
farmers and leveraging ICT, and provides an opportunity to offer a basket of
services including transaction banking to various stakeholders, while spreading
risk across various stakeholders of the agri-value chain. Additionally, the IAFP

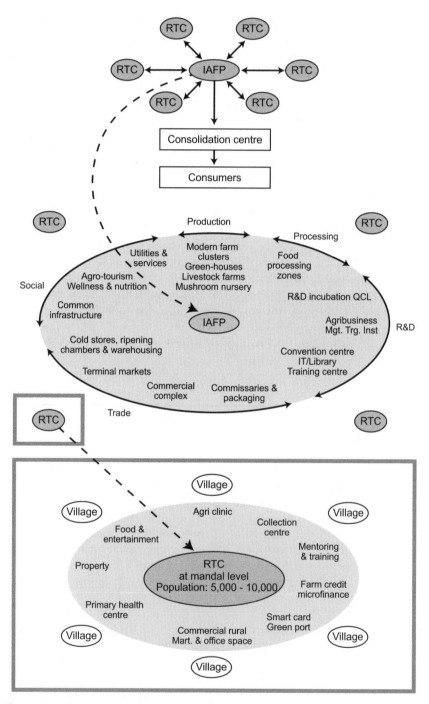

Figure 5.6 Integrated agricultural food park model and activities
Source: case authors, Poosapati and Chakravathy

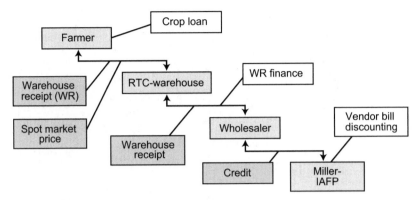

Figure 5.7 Customized financial products for edible oil processing value chain stakeholders
Source: case authors, Poosapati and Chakravathy

offers a gamut of non-financial services, thus enhancing credit recovery by providing several non-financial services to the farmers as depicted in Figure 5.8.

YES BANK has found that the advantages of the IAFP value chain integration can work well even when producers are very small. The advantages presented by the IAFP model are portrayed in Figure 5.9 with the case of the integrated dairy facility of very small dairy producers. By pooling their cows to

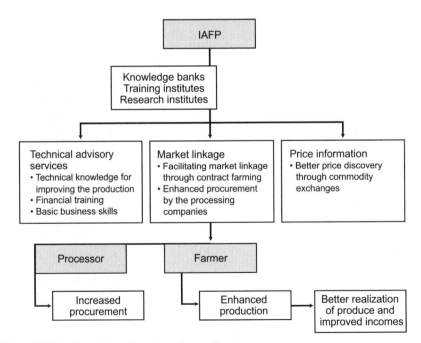

Figure 5.8 Non-financial services favouring credit recovery
Source: case authors, Poosapati and Chakravathy

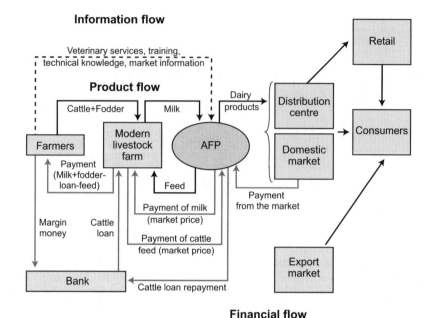

Figure 5.9 Integrated dairy at IAFP: information, product and financial flow
Source: case authors, Poosapati and Chakravathy

form an economically competitive dairy farm, they not only achieve economies of scale but can be integrated with the services and markets to achieve
higher quality products and higher incomes for the many families involved.

By virtue of its enabling structure of IAFP, synergy between various components and participants of the dairy value chain, augmented by ready availability of inputs (improved cattle breeds and fodder/feed and equipment and
supplies for the processing units), information (technical and market information) and value chain finance (loan secured by product flow, term loans and
others), and assured off-take (forward tie-ups with the retailers and processors
in the domestic and international markets), the integrated dairy facility provides uninterrupted flows of knowledge, product and finance while impeding
value losses in the dairy value chain.

Conclusion

As explained, the IAFP is an *innovative value creating business structure* designed
to offer specific technical know-how, customized financial products, state-of-
the-art infrastructure and marketing solutions to its stakeholders, thus addressing major value chain inefficiencies and effectively mitigating risks associated
with the Indian agriculture. The self sustainable model, together with the government interventions of regulatory reforms, infrastructural development and

financial incentives to encourage participation of agribusiness corporations, creates a win–win scenario for all stakeholders. The model provides farmers market opportunities, higher prices and economy of scale benefits not feasible in isolation, thereby substantially increasing net earnings.

Successful replication of such models across strategic production hubs for key agricultural commodities can lead to the transition of Indian agriculture and processed food industry from an unorganized, supply-driven, low-value business scenario to an exceedingly well organized, high-tech and safe, demand-led, and high-value orientation with substantial employment perspectives, averaging an estimated direct employment of 8,000 and indirect employment of 30,000 people per IAFP. YES BANK, along with its strategic partners, is leveraging the experience and expertise gained during implementation of the IAFP model in India and intends to implement the unique concept in South East Asian and African countries, with each one done after developing a tailor-made model catering to the specific needs and requirements of the country.

While pioneering in its integrated and knowledge banking value chain approach, YES BANK remains committed to its clients across the entire agri-value chain and contributing towards farmer empowerment and entrepreneurial development, and thus transforming Indian 'agriculture' to 'agribusiness'.

Case references

www.yesbank.in [accessed 4 October 2009].

CHAPTER 6
Lessons learned and summary recommendations

Value chain finance has been implemented in many countries across regions at varying stages of development, and with differences in their financial systems and enabling environments. Some of the learning and recommendations described in this chapter are drawn from specific experiences in Africa, Asia, Latin America, the Middle East or Eastern Europe. Nevertheless, it is possible and useful to generalize the learning for the successful utilization of value chain finance in a range of circumstances and environments. Therefore, the application of the lessons learned may require further refinement and adaptation depending upon the context, the characteristics of the value chain, and the conditions that impact the borrower and lender. Although some of the lessons learned and recommendations may appear obvious to experienced professionals, the authors have attempted to be comprehensive to benefit new entrants to the field who are using this publication as a primer for work in value chain finance.

Lessons learned

Value chain finance is a comprehensive and holistic 'approach'. First and foremost, agricultural value chain finance is not simply a single instrument or a defined 'recipe' to follow. It involves systemic analysis of an entire value chain and the relationship amongst its actors. This holistic approach enables stakeholders to design financial interventions that may incorporate one or various financial instruments. The approach enables lenders to better evaluate creditworthiness of individuals or groups of businesses within the chain through identifying risks and analysing the competitiveness of that chain. A value chain finance approach is already used by some leading financial institutions that include sector analysis and market potential in their lending programmes. It focuses on the transactions throughout the chain which is quite dissimilar in approach to the majority of financial institutions which offer a relatively fixed set of loan products secured by the collateral of a specific borrower with little consideration given to the market system as a whole.

Value chain finance can be 'positive-sum'. The use of contractual agreements is increasingly important in modern value chains. The strength of these contracts and the commitment of the partners to abide by them is a key determining factor in the success of value chain financing. When contract commitment is strong, additional funds can flow into the chain while the asset value of the products in the chain remains. The challenge, however, is to build the understanding, capacity and regulatory environment to ensure that commitments are obeyed.

The viability of value chain finance depends on 'insider knowledge'. The drivers of a value chain, who are often the businesses involved in the processing and marketing of agricultural outputs, know the business and the other actors in the chain in a way the financial institutions by themselves cannot. This information gap is exacerbated by lack of transparency in many countries, where balance sheets presented to financial institutions may not be reliable and business risks are often hidden. While not resolving this underlying problem with a chain approach, banks have more reference points for financial and technical information which can reduce risk. As a result, they may also be more willing to lend to small farmers, traders and others in the chain about whom they do not have enough knowledge to be confident in lending otherwise. For example, by observing that reputable and successful processing or marketing firms have entered into informal or contractual relationships with small farmers, financiers are reassured of the creditworthiness of the producers and are more likely to lend to them.

Financing efficiency and risk reduction can be achieved by financing through the strongest chain actor or actors. By financing the stronger, less risky agribusinesses, most often those near the end of the chain, the financial costs associated with risk protection are reduced. In this way, a financial institution can lend to an established business such as a processor, and let the processor make internal value chain lending decisions based on their first-hand knowledge of producers or traders. In addition, the transaction costs for lending to the larger entities is generally much less for the financial institution, and the primary borrower manages the lower cost of on-lending to multiple smaller entities.

Weakness at any link in the chain can increase financing risk at all levels. Value chain finance decisions derive from the health of the chain or sector, including its cash and commodity flows, rather than relying on traditional collateral. This means that the level of mutual interest for the common good within the chain can reduce risk, but only if that interest is genuine and the linkages are strong. Even when a particular business is extremely stable and risk free, if their behaviour jeopardizes others in the chain, then value chain financing will not result in productive outcomes. Although this is a self-evident statement, when one is dealing in agricultural value chains that may not have collateral as the basis for lending at the foundation of the chain, awareness of these dynamics must be explicit in a facilitator's or lender's analysis.

Industry competitiveness is a must for those within the sub-sector to receive finance. A good client in a declining sub-sector or in one that exhibits an increasingly obsolete technology or technical capacity is a poor investment risk. A value chain approach makes it incumbent on a lender or investor to consider the competitiveness of the industry. It is no longer sufficient to know that a piece of collateral is available if the loan fails, but there is a shared responsibility to assess the supply of resources, efficiencies in production and value addition, capacity of value chain actors, access to technology, and economies of scale issues. If there are weaknesses, value chain businesses may be able to fix them in a timely fashion, or a financier might decide to move to new sub-sectors that are more competitive and therefore the businesses within them are better credit risks. For example, it is well known that good agricultural practices (GAP), hazard analysis and critical control point (HACCP), traceability and other industry regulated standards and norms have transformed the international fruit and vegetable business. Many producers are unable to meet such standards, and the value chains within which they operate are no longer competitive.

Value chain development depends on a range of supports and services. Understanding that value chain functioning and industry competitiveness are critical to successful value chain finance is not enough. The actual implementation of additional value chain development activities may be warranted in some cases. In the integrated model presented in the introduction, holistic development of the chain is a priority, with finance as one essential service in that process. In particular, where the goal is the integration of smallholder farmers, a range of services, sometimes referred to as an 'ecosystem', may be required, these include: business and technical training, access to inputs, group organizing,

Figure 6.1 Farmer-centric ecosystem services
Source: Rutten (2007)

building negotiation skills, dispute resolution and collective bargaining skills, market information and access, and infrastructure support from warehouses to transportation and communication as shown in Figure 6.1. Value chain development goes far beyond the expertise and capacity of financial institutions, although these issues are integral to successful value chain financing and therefore should inform financing decisions. Since financial institutions cannot provide this range of services themselves, they may need to determine if the required services are available and if linkages or partnerships are possible and desirable. Frequently, it is a facilitating organization developing a value chain that approaches a lending institution to support the overall work with the financial component of the solution.

Agricultural value chain finance does not replace conventional finance. Value chain financing is both *to and through* the chain, and therefore depends, at least in part, on conventional sources and services of financing to the chain. The relationship and levels of intervention of financing are often the factors that change in conventional bank finance – closer information flow and interaction, indirect financing for some clients, point of sale financial arrangements, etc. A second point to note is that value chain financing is very focused in its use. It is directed specifically to chain activities and is largely short-term financing; household and agricultural needs for financial services are diverse and multifunctional and require financial services that go beyond value chain financing.

A well rounded, but weighted assessment of borrowers is critical. While using the value chain to evaluate risk, it is still necessary to assess the capacity of the specific borrowers. As described in the introduction, criteria such as the 5 C's of lending can be useful tools in determining the creditworthiness of clients. However, under a value chain approach increased weight is given to the last two 'Cs' – conditions and cash flow – as opposed to the first three of character, capacity and collateral. The health of the value chain as well as the cash and product flows of the clients within the chain are critical for success. Thus, risk appraisal requires assessment of these factors while taking into account how the risk impacts the specific borrower, or set of borrowers, who are being evaluated for a loan.

Embedding finance can increase access and efficiency. Formal loan processes can be costly and time consuming, and this may hinder access to finance for some value chain businesses, including farmers. Internal value chain finance allows for the inclusion of finance in a package of inputs and/or other services that flow through the chain. This type of embedded financial service can lead to both improved efficiencies and repayment, although there can also be a lack of transparency regarding the cost of funds or inputs/services that leads to abuses. However, embedded finance is one of the oldest forms of value chain finance, and in general the interest of the 'client' is served through being able to access such a comprehensive package of inputs, services and finance.

Technological innovation is important in financing value chain businesses. New technologies have opened the door for growth in the use of value chain financing, and inclusion of even remote and small producers. Easier communication via mobile phones and the Internet facilitate sales transactions, price information and money transfers, while better MIS systems allow for even small financial institutions to offer the flexible disbursements and payments needed in value chain finance. However, current availability and access to technology is very unequal, and cannot be leveraged in all contexts. As technology development and availability are rapidly evolving, stakeholders in a chain will benefit from awareness of changes that can lead to phenomenal advancements in very short timeframes (e.g. M-PESA).

Diversification and other mechanisms that mitigate the concentration of risk in a value chain activity are important. Caution is also noted regarding a singular focus on any one sector or value chain by a financial institution. While specialization is an important ingredient in achieving competitiveness, it also has associated risks for both the businesses within the chain as well as the financiers who would support it. Unless risks are adequately mitigated, over-reliance on a single chain or market can unduly increase the risks related to uncontrollable factors such as global price fluctuations, industry turns and natural disasters, including drought and hurricanes. Price hedging, insurance and market awareness can mitigate sector risk but a need for diversification of product lines and target markets may also be necessary. This is important for producers and processors as well as for banks and all financiers. For the latter, it is critical to recognize this risk both as part of their clients' financial assessment as well as of their own portfolio assessment.

Business models can influence the selection and application of financial instruments. The type and structure of the business model (e.g. producer driven, lead firm, etc., described above) influence the selection and application of instruments used in value chain financing. Understanding the model and its drivers can help those providing finance be aware of the chain relationships and make appropriate decisions regarding financing. Some instruments can be used in weak chains but others, such as receivables finance, require models where the linkages are strong and secure. The models are also influenced by the products themselves, with some chains being more difficult to integrate and/or requiring more direction and control to be exerted by a lead firm.

Value chain finance reflects values of stakeholder participation. The most sophisticated financial instruments contain incentives or shared risks amongst stakeholders. Islamic banking in some of its various forms similarly involves borrower–lender shared risks and returns. The underlying concept of mutuality is traditional but relevant to formal financing since the higher the level of shared risks and returns, the stronger the relationship tends to be. In this way, for example, clear benchmark formulae for price determination based upon the market conditions (e.g. some element of shared price increase flexibility) result in more lasting relationships than those with inflexible fixed prices, whereby 'side-selling' or reneging on purchases often result when market prices change. The importance of shared interest extends beyond financing to the healthy functioning of the value chain itself.

Application of value chain finance instruments depends upon the enabling environment. The flexibility, lack of reliance on traditional collateral and evolving nature of value chain finance makes it complex for policymakers to understand and central bankers to regulate and supervise. A weak or insufficient legal structure legal structure in many countries means that the full range of value chain finance instruments is not available. For example, several of the instruments described here, such as factoring and leasing, are relatively recent introductions in some countries and require new laws in order to be implemented. Other instruments, such as warehouse receipts require regulatory revisions for the acceptance of new forms of collateral, as well as having in place grading standards and adequate storage facilities. Public and private entities must collaborate on research and development to understand these instruments, and their implications for policies and supervision in their specific context. Fortunately, lessons and examples are available, and the experiences in some countries can serve to inform and guide the policy development in others.

Value chain finance clients need financial services beyond credit. The effective support of value chain businesses from smallholders through to processors and retailers recognizes that finance is not just a loan. Smallholders in particular have often been overlooked in the provision of a broad range of financial services that include savings, insurance and lines of credit. Not all these financial services are, nor need to be, provided by formal banking institutions. For example, savings and credit groups can play a role in financing, organizing and empowering many smallholders to integrate into value chains. At the same time, community-led social funds and even traders can serve the needs of producers in times of personal or financial crisis. However, more and more microfinance institutions and banks are developing approaches to offer agricultural insurance, health insurance and savings products, and the services of commodity management companies are growing to provide guidance, security and support throughout the chain.

Smallholder facilitation and capacity building can lead to competitiveness. Value chain integration and the increasingly stringent consumer requirements exclude many small farmers, traders and agribusinesses. Yet, with sufficient technical, organizational and/or business capacity building they can become competitive in many markets, and thereby improve incomes and access to financing. Often, facilitation is helpful or required to provide the support and links into strong chains. This can come from chain operators, third party development agencies and government.

Regional differences are less important than a country's level of development. The applications of value chain models, as well as the accompanying financial tools, are not substantially different from one region to the next. For example, a global financial institution does not change the way it undertakes financing of a value chain nor does the application of warehouse receipts or trader finance differ significantly by region, even though, as was seen, the relative importance of who provides the financing within a chain may change by region and commodity. The level of development of a country's financial markets is quite important in determining which financial tools can be used, either because the regulatory environment supports its use, or there is an increased use of particular types of value chain finance as an alternative precisely because conventional financial markets are weak. The presence and use of commodity exchanges, which are most active in larger, developed countries for certain commodities, are important determinants for the use of some of the value chain finance instruments. There is also heterogeneity related to the nature of the product chain as some chains lend themselves to higher levels of value addition and integration (e.g. sugar cane) whereas with others (e.g. maize) there is more difficulty consolidating chains. However, the value chain financing approach – comprehensively assessing and knowing the chain and structuring financial interventions accordingly – is applicable in all regions.

Many challenges remain. Side-selling and other forms of contract breaking remain a formidable hurdle to overcome in financing through value chains. Successful models of value chain financing at the beginning of the chain have often required up-front support in organization, training and confidence building for ensuring strong linkages and commitment among the actors in the chain. Payment of those support services, especially for small farmers and small agribusiness companies, is an ongoing challenge for both the public and private sectors.

Summary of recommendations

Value chain financing is recommended as a promising approach for increasing financing to agriculture at all levels of the chain. More learning and a deeper analysis is required for addressing key constraining factors. Most important among these is research to help improve: 1) improved policies and regulation for some of the value chain finance instruments; 2) approaches for optimal financial inclusion; and 3) contract enforcement. In addition, greater dissemination of the experiences and learning is needed in the universities, banking institutes and among development agencies and governments.

This volume includes case studies and analysis throughout that provides pointers to financial institutions, value chain stakeholders, including facilitating organizations and policymakers. Additional recommendations can be derived from the lessons learned. The authors encourage any who are interested in pursuing agricultural value chain financing approaches to carefully review the above sections which provide the context for the following recommendations. The recommendations in this section coalesce this learning and offer a summary guideline.

Recommendations regarding financial institutions

These recommendations are designed to inform:

- Lending institutions that endeavour to take value chain dynamics into account when providing loans to specific businesses or types of business within a given chain.
- Financial institutions that aim to support the development of value chains, potentially at multiple levels, through appropriate loan products and possibly other financial instruments.
- Facilitating organizations that work with financial institutions to either strengthen the institution or to extend financial services to under serviced agricultural sub-sectors.

Confidence in market demand. Market driven value chains have proven to be the most efficient ones. Agribusinesses that seek financing need, at minimum, an understanding of market demand and how their outputs are positioned to respond to that demand. In the case where greater value chain integration exists, businesses may be linked to a lead firm with a reliable market or established market linkages. Although lending institutions may not have the competence to assess market demand, they should have confidence in the capacity of the borrower to do so.

Leverage the knowledge of value chain businesses. Value chain firms themselves are often the best source of knowledge regarding the functioning of the chain and the various businesses within it. This knowledge enables such firms to reduce risks, and to make decisions about internal value chain financing versus formal agricultural lending. By leveraging the knowledge and experience of successful value chain firms, financial institutions are better situated to make wise financing decisions.

Contribute to value chain strengthening. Financial institutions have the potential to contribute to the strengthening of value chains through building knowledge and supporting the development of needed services. Rather than investing in one component of the chain, the financial institution can grow expertise in the chain, share this knowledge, and provide financing to support services. This not only benefits clients, but also expands lending opportunities while lowering risks.

Multiply financial products to meet needs. Value chains require a variety of loan products as well as other financial services such as savings and insurance. In order to strengthen businesses, reduce risks, and create a healthy financial system, it is important to investigate the financial needs of value chain firms from farmers to retailers. Unorthodox products, tailor-made adaptations and innovative approaches may hold the greatest promise for developing the chain and supporting finance.

Strengthen risk assessment and lending criteria. Value chains offer a structure and relationships that have great potential to reduce the risk of agricultural lending. It is incumbent on the financial institution to evaluate risk and to take into consideration conventional criteria along with new criteria that encompass value chain knowledge and functioning. These include:

- knowledge of actors and market;
- risk management systems;
- transaction costs of delivering financial products;
- governance systems;
- observance of contracts;
- capacity to establish alliances;
- availability of inputs, services and other supports.

Realize that finance is not enough. Finance is often one of many needs in a business. Even though finance is often a necessary requirement in successful value chains, finance alone is generally not sufficient. The business development services associated with value chains or market development may be more important to success than the financial inputs. Being aware of the gaps and opportunities in a value chain, and promoting partnerships and ways to address hurdles that go beyond the capacity of the financial institution to resolve can improve the results of the value chain partners and those who finance them.

Investigate the application of new technologies. New technologies offer lower cost solutions for hard-to-reach clients, as well as methods to form networks, exchange information and monitor flows of money. This is common in microfinance and other financial services as well; what is less evident is that new technologies in food chain industries can also quickly affect specific sectors and be a barrier to those who cannot react to the new demands.

Recommendations regarding value chain stakeholders

These recommendations are designed to inform:

- Agribusinesses such as lead firms that participate in a value chain, and need to evaluate lending and borrowing opportunities from a holistic perspective.
- Service providers who support a value chain – e.g. transporters, telecommunications, packagers, equipment suppliers – who would like to understand the viability of the chain, and therefore the risks involved in offering credit to value chain businesses or taking loans to service the chain.

- Facilitating organizations that work with smallholder farmers, agribusinesses, service providers and other stakeholders to strengthen the value chain in general.

Understand market demand. This is the primary consideration for any value chain stakeholder or facilitator. As noted earlier, market-driven value chains have proven to be the most efficient ones. Value chain businesses must understand market demand and how the chain's outputs are positioned to respond to that demand. A lead firm has the unique opportunity to not only understand this demand, but to convey it to others in the chain to ensure responsive production and value-adding activities.

Share knowledge. In traditional systems, knowledge was often not shared due to fear of losing market competitiveness. In today's global markets, knowledge is key to maintaining one's position in the market. In the past, traders were often very secretive and kept information away from farmers at the bottom of the chain, preferring to reduce risk and ensure profit by squeezing prices rather than building markets. Now, when producers understand what is demanded, and how to respond to market trends, the chain and therefore the lead firm, intermediaries and service providers are all in a better position to succeed.

Be aware of value chain needs. As a stakeholder in a value chain, it becomes necessary to understand the needs of the chain, and not just those of one's own business. Constraints may be financial or non-financial, and they may affect many or just a few. Understanding these issues and how one can mitigate risks is essential. This knowledge can lead to increased cooperation with other stakeholders, and bolstering of the value chain in general.

Develop business alliances. The capacity to develop lasting relationships that are mutually beneficial is a characteristic of durable value chain businesses. In forming relationships, one must consider the incentives for all parties concerned to participate in the relationship – both financial and non-financial – and how an alliance fits into the overall functioning of a value chain.

Develop competitive industries through cooperation. Globalization has put greater pressure on individual businesses to be part of competitive industries. Building on shared knowledge and cooperation, value chain businesses can develop solid market linkages, long-term buying relationships, agreed upon standards, brand recognition, and access to appropriate technical skills and technologies. Without this type of collaboration, businesses are likely to fail in the face of stiff competition from other better functioning value chains.

Build associations and other supports. One mechanism noted for developing a competitive industry was through an industry association. Associations provide a structure for sharing information, promoting best practices, accessing markets (e.g. trade fairs), lobbying for policy change, forming alliances, developing brands (e.g. Egyptian cotton) and other forms of collaboration. Associations may consist of sub-groups like exporters or producers, or have broad-based memberships that welcome those who support the industry such as marketers, accountants and consultants.

Recommendations regarding policymakers

These recommendations are designed to inform:

- Policymakers who are interested in supporting the development and competitiveness of value chains and the businesses within those chains.
- Value chain stakeholders and financial institutions that seek to influence policymakers by providing reliable information on value chain functioning, success factors and results.
- Facilitating organizations that are developing value chains, supporting the stakeholders, or building related financial systems, and endeavour to influence the enabling environment.

Infrastructure is a critical need. Agricultural communities often lack the infrastructure that would enable them to thrive and contribute to a nation's food security and/or exports. Too often, there are gaps in basic services: inadequate electricity for operating machinery and processing equipment, lack of storage facilities to ensure product quality, undeveloped road systems to promote fast delivery and reduced spoilage, no greenhouse structures to prolong seasons and increase yields, and insufficient water and technologies for irrigation and other farm activities. It is costly and policymakers must make agriculture a priority to overcome these obstacles.

Support legislation. Policymakers have a critical role to play in the creation of enabling environments. Legislation may target financing issues from the regulations that govern microfinance institutions to those that support the development of managed warehouses that enable collateralization of inventory. Alternatively, legislation can support the certification of agricultural inputs, the registration of agribusinesses, the development of industry standards, the opening of domestic and international markets, and a host of other supporting regulations for agricultural sub-sectors. For value chain stakeholders, facilitators and policymakers, understanding the regulatory bottlenecks, and how to overcome them, can result in significant changes in legislation and the enabling environment.

Consider a value chain lens in agricultural development. In delivering governmental support to agricultural development – for example, expansion of extension services, investment in agricultural research, development of wholesale markets – it is useful to employ a value chain lens. Too often, well intentioned government initiatives are disconnected from the reality on the ground. Such efforts can be enhanced by building suitable public and private alliances for planning and implementation, as outlined in the next point.

Build supportive alliances. With the intensification of agricultural value chains, there are new alternatives for developing the agricultural economy. It is important to bridge the gap between public and private sector plans and strategies, involving all actors from farmers, to agribusinesses, traders, financiers and government. At the same time, there is a need to complement the government extension machinery; this second agriculture revolution needs active participation from all actors, besides the government. Policymakers can take an active role in leading this collaboration.

Contribute to risk mitigation. Policymakers that aim to invest in their country's agricultural development can utilize funds to assist in reducing risk in financing agriculture and agro-industry. For example, government funds can be used to support guarantee funds, agricultural insurance or incentives for start-up. Each of these has to be assessed in light of the agricultural goals of the country, the nature of the funds and the long-term impact and viability; using funds in this way may catalyse agricultural finance and investment and promote the development of competitive agricultural value chains and efficient financial markets which support them. Introduction of legislative innovation, such as the rural product notes in Brazil, that provide access to advance funds on forward contracts and allow that disputes can be rapidly settled in out-of-court settlements, can be considered as an example of increasing access to finance and reducing risks of moral hazard.

Training and capacity building. The concepts and many of the instruments of value chain financing are not well understood. Universities, bank training institutes and development organizations must be encouraged to develop the training and teaching curricula needed to build the capacity required.

Understand the limitations of value chain finance. Two cautions must be understood. Firstly, value chain integration may not be good for all those involved. The least powerful in the chain may become marginalized in certain value chains. Value chain finance cannot address inequities that may be inherent in some value chain relationships. Governance through policies and enforcement is required. Secondly, value chain finance can only address financial needs related to the chain; the conditions for promoting broad-based financial services to all households and businesses must also be pursued.

List of conferences

AFRACA Agribanks Forum: *Africa Value Chain Financing*, Nairobi, Kenya, 16–19, October, 2007, presentations available from: www.ruralfinance.org/id/54740 [accessed 4 October 2009].

Asia International Conference: *Agri Revolution: Financing the Agricultural Value Chain*, Mumbai, India, 15–17 March, 2007, presentations available from: www.ruralfinance.org/id/48291 [accessed 4 October 2009].

Global Agro-Industries Forum: *Improving Competitiveness and Development Impact*, New Delhi, India, 8–11 April, 2008, further information from: www.gaif08.org/ [accessed 4 October 2009].

Latin American Conference: *Agricultural Value Chain Finance*, Costa Rica, 16–18 May, 2006, summary of conference available from: www.ruralfinance.org/id/54079 [accessed 4 October 2009].

Southeast Asia Regional Conference: *Agricultural Value Chain Financing*, Kuala Lumpur, Malaysia, 12–14 December, 2007, conference proceedings available from: www.ruralfinance.org/id/68010 [accessed 4 October 2009].

References

Please refer to the above list of conferences to view the presentations cited in the following references.

Actis (2007) 'Africa agribusiness fund', presentation at the AFRACA Agribanks Forum.

Agrawal, S. (2007) 'Weather risk: technical assistance for rural development', presentation at the Asia International Conference.

Alcantara, D. (2006) 'Banco do Brasil: financial institutions and agricultural value chains', presentation at the Latin American Conference.

Ananthakrishnan, P.V. (2007) 'Structured finance through collateral management', presentation at the Asia International Conference.

Balakrishnan, R. (2007) 'Poor reach, poor repayment: problems with agricultural finance in India and NABARD's plans to tackle them', presentation at the Asia International Conference.

Boily, Y. and Julien, P. (2007) 'Roles of the SACCOS network in value chain finance', presentation at the AFRACA Agribanks Forum.

Campaigne, J. (2007) 'Financing the agricultural value supply chain', presentation at the AFRACA Agribanks Forum.

Campion, A. (2006) 'Agricultural value chain finance in Peru', presentation at the Latin American Conference.

Campion, A. (2007) 'Technical assistance, risk mitigation and access to financial services: Agromantaro', in R. Quirós (ed.) *Summary of the Conference: Agricultural Value Chain Finance*, pp. 124–128, FAO and Academia de Centroamérica, San José, [online] www.ruralfinance.org/id/54079 [accessed 24 September 2009]

Cavalini, J. (2007) 'Hortifruiti', in R. Quirós (ed.) *Summary of the Conference: Agricultural Value Chain Finance*, pp. 69–73, FAO and Academia de Centroamérica, San José, available from: www.ruralfinance.org/id/54079 [accessed 24 September 2009]

Chávez, R. (2006) 'Esquema Parafinanciero – UNIPRO, presentation at the Latin American Conference.

Cherogony, M. (2007) 'IFAD's experience in value chain financing in east and southern Africa', presentation at the Latin American Conference.

Choudhary, A. K. (2007) 'Field warehousing and the role of a collateral management agency', presentation at the Asia International Conference.

Consultative Group for Assistance to the Poorest (CGAP) (2009) *Poor People Using Mobile Financial Services: Observations on Customer Usage and Impact from M-Pesa*, CGAP Brief, August 2009, World Bank, Washington D.C.

Coop, D. (2008) *Striving Toward a Competitive Industry: The Importance of Dynamic Value Chain Facilitation*, USAID MicroReport #140, USAID, Washington D.C.

Corrales, L. (2006) 'BN desarrollo: promoviendo las cadenas agrícolas de valor', presentation at the Latin American Conference.

Da Silva, C. (2007) 'Improving small farmers' access to finance: the pros and cons of contract farming', presentation at the Asia International Conference.

Da Silva, C.A., Baker, D., Shephered, A.W., Miranda-da-Cruz, S. and Jeanae, C. (eds) (2009) *Agro-industries for development*, FAO,UNIDO,IFAD and CABI.

Das, P.K. and Baria, B.G. (2005) *Increasing the Flow of Credit to Agriculture by the Commercial Banks in India – The Task Ahead*, IBA Bulletin, October 2005: 18–24.

Díaz, R. (2008) *Fortalecimiento operativo del MAG para responder a las demandas de las agrocadenas estratégicas regionales y nacionales*, Centro Internacional de Política Económica, universidad Nacional, (unpublished).

Digal, L. (2009) *Southeast Asia Regional Conference On Agricultural Value Chain Financing Conference Proceedings*, Kuala Lumpur, Malaysia, 12–14 December, 2007, Asian Productivity Organization (APO), National Productivity Council and FAO, Rome. [online] www.ruralfinance.org/id/68010 [accessed 25 September 2009]

E-Choupal (2008) 'Improving competitiveness and development impact', presentation at the Global Agro-Industries Forum.

FAO Bulletin (1992) *Food and Agriculture Organization of the United Nations Bulletin*, FAO, Rome, Italy.

Farm Concern International (2008) www.familyconcern.net [accessed 2 October 2009]

Food and Agriculture Organization (FAO) (2009) FAO of the United Nations unpublished project document project: GCP/NER/041/BEL

Fries, B. (2007) 'The value chain framework, rural finance, and lessons for TA providers and donors', presentation at the Asia International Conference.

Fries, R. and Akin, B. (2004) *Value Chains and Their Significance for Addressing the Rural Finance Challenge*, USAID MicroReport # 20, USAID, Washington, D.C.

Gallardo, J.S. (1997) *World Bank Report*, Washington D.C.

Gálvez, E. (2006a) 'Financiamiento del comercio agrícola en América Latina', presentation at the Latin American Conference.

Gálvez, E. (2006b) 'Financiación de la comercialización agrícola en América Latina', *Documento ocasional del servicio de gestión, comercialización y finanzas agrícolas 10*, FAO, Rome.

Ghore, Y. (2007) *Agri-Revolution Conference: Financing the Agricultural Value Chain, Conference Summary Report*, Mumbai, India.

Gonzalez-Vega, C. (2006) 'Modern value chains: toward the creation and strengthening of creditworthiness', in Quirós, R. (ed.) (2007) *Agricultural value chain finance*, FAO and Academia de Centroamérica, pp. 45–63, San José, available from: www.ruralfinance.org/id/54079 [accessed 4 October 2009]

Harper, M. (ed.) (2008) *Inclusive Value Chains in India: Linking the Smallest Farmers to Producers*, World Scientific Publishing, Singapore.

Hegbe, B. (2007) 'End to end financing in the agriculture and livestock sector', presentation at the Asia International Conference.

International Finance Corporation (IFC) (2009) Global Trade Finance Program www.ifc.org/GTFP [last accessed 1 July, 2009]

Johnston, C. and Meyer, R. (2008) 'Value chain governance and access to finance: maize, sugar cane and sunflower oil in Uganda', *Enterprise Development and Microfinance* 19(4): 281, Practical Action Publishing, Rugby.

Jones, L.M. (ed.) (2009) *Value Chains and Development: Emerging Theory and Practice*, Practical Action Publishing, Rugby.

Kimathi, M., Nandazi, N.M., Miller, C. and Kipsang, D.N.K. (2007) *Africa Value Chain Financing, 3rd AFRACA Agribanks Synthesis report*, AFRACA and FAO, Nairobi, Kenya.

Klapper, L. (2005) *The Role of 'Reverse Factoring' in Supplier Financing of Small and Medium Sized Enterprises*, World Bank, Washington D.C.

Kloeppinger-Todd, R. (2007), 'Leasing as credit alternative', presentation at the Asia International Conference.

Law, J. and Smullen, J. (eds) (2008) *Dictionary of Finance and Banking*, Oxford University Press, Oxford.

Lazaro, P. (2007) 'Sustainable logistics development program', in Digal, L. (ed.) (2009) *Southeast Asia Regional Conference on Agricultural Value Chain Financing Conference Proceedings*, Asian Productivity Organization, National Productivity Council and FAO, Rome, available from: www.ruralfinance. org/id/68010 [accessed 4 October 2009]

Mangabat, M. (2007) 'The role of financial institutions in value chains', presentation at the Southeast Asian Conference.

Marangu, K. (2007) 'Kenya BDS program, experience in value chain facilitation', presentation at the AFRACA Agribanks Forum.

Martinez, E. (2006) 'Banorte Banca agropecuaria', presentation at the Latin America Conference.

Medlicott, A. (2006) 'Modern value chains: toward the creation and strengthening of creditworthiness', in R. Quirós (ed.) (2007) *Summary of the Conference: Agricultural Value Chain Finance*, pp. 119–121, FAO and Academia de Centroamérica, San José, available from: www.ruralfinance.org/id/54079 [accessed 24 September 2009]

Melosevic, C. (2006) 'Models of value chain finance', in R. Quirós (ed.) *Summary of the Conference: Agricultural Value Chain Finance*, pp. 74–76, FAO and Academia de Centroamérica, San José, available from: www.ruralfinance. org/id/54079 [accessed 24 September 2009]

Miehlbradt, A. and Jones, L. (2007) *A market research toolkit for value chain initiatives, information for action: A toolkit series for market development practitioners*, MEDA publications.

Miller, C. (2007a) 'Financing along the supply chain: setting the stage', presentation at the Asia International Conference.

Miller, C. (2007b) 'Value chain financing models – building collateral and improving credit worthiness', paper and presentation at the Southeast Asian Conference, paper in Digal, L. (ed.) (2009) *Southeast Asia Regional Conference on Agricultural Value Chain Financing Conference Proceedings*, Asian Productivity Organization, National Productivity Council and FAO, Rome, available from: www.ruralfinance.org/id/68010 [accessed 4 October 2009]

Miller, C. (2008a) 'A bakers's dozen lessons of value chain financing in agriculture', *Enterprise Development and Microfinance* 19(4), Practical Action Publishing, Rugby.

Miller, C. (2008b) 'Finance using linkages and value chains', NENARACA Seminar on *Rural Finance – Expanding the Frontier*, Sana'a, Yemen, May 5–8, 2008, referencing O. Imady, and D.H. Dieter Seibel, *Principles and Products of Islamic Finance*, University of Cologne, Development Research Center (unpublished).

Miller, C. and da Silva, C. (2007) 'Value chain financing in agriculture', *Enterprise Development and Microfinance* 13(2/3), Practical Action Publishing, Rugby.

Minae, S. and Khisa, G. (2007) 'Farmer field schools', presentation at the AFRACA Agribanks Forum.

Ministry of Agriculture, Government of India (2009) http://agricoop.nic.in/ [accessed 1 September, 2009]

Mrema, H. (2007) 'Mainstreaming smallholder farmers into the world economy, using farmer ownership model', presentation at the AFRACA Agribanks Forum.

Muiruri, E. (2007) 'Strategic partnership for finance', presentation at the AFRACA Agribanks Forum.

Mwangi, K. (2007) 'Value chain financing models and vision for value chain financing in Africa', presentation at the AFRACA Agribanks Forum.

Myint, K. (2007) 'Value chain finance', presentation at Asia International Conference.

Nair, A. (2007) 'Financing agriculture: risks and risk management strategies', presentation at the AFRACA Agribanks Forum.

Natarajan, R. (2007) 'SNX, an electronic spot exchange for fruits and vegetables', presentation at Asia International Conference.

National Bank for Agriculture and Rural Development (NABARD) (2009) *2008–09 Annual Report* [online] www.nabard.org/financialsreports.asp [accessed 29 September 2009]

Nyoro, J. (2007) 'Financing agriculture: Historical perspective', presentation at the AFRACA Agribanks Forum.

Odo, G. (2007) 'Effective ways to reach smallholders', presentation at the AFRACA Agribanks Forum.

Park, W.S. (2007) 'Agriculture finance and marketing systems in Korea', presentation at the Asia International Conference.

Prasittipayong, P. (2007) 'The case of value chain financing in the shrimp industry in Thailand', in Digal, L. (2009) *Southeast Asia Regional Conference On Agricultural Value Chain Financing Conference Proceedings*, Kuala Lumpur, Malaysia, 12–14 December, 2007, Asian Productivity Organization (APO), National Productivity Council and FAO, Rome, available from: www.ruralfinance.org/id/68010 [accessed 25 September 2009]

Quirós, R. (ed.) (2007) *Agricultural value chain finance*, FAO and Academia de Centroamérica, San José.

Ramana, N.V. (2007a) 'Lessons from the field', presentation at the Asia International Conference.

Ramana, N. (2007b) 'Financial services to poor farmers: a proper mix of instruments, risks and rewards', presentation at the Asia International Conference.

Romero, R. (2006) 'Chestnut Hill Farms', presentation at the Latin American Conference.

Rutten, L., Choudhary, A. and Sinha, A. (2007) 'Building a new agriculture trade, finance and risk management system', presentation at the Asia International Conference.

Salenque, A. (2007) 'An effective way to integrate small-scale farmers in the value chain: the experience of BRAC', in Digal (2009) *Southeast Asia Regional Conference On Agricultural Value Chain Financing Conference Proceedings*, Asia, Asian Productivity Organization, National Productivity Council and FAO, Rome, available from: www.ruralfinance.org/id/68010 [accessed 4 October 2009]

Shepherd, A.W. (2004) 'Financing agricultural marketing, the Asian experience', *Agricultural management, marketing and finance occasional paper No.2*, FAO, Rome.

Shwedel, K. (2007) 'Value chain financing: a strategy for an orderly, competitive, integrated market', available from: www.ruralfinance.org/id/54079 [accessed 24 September 2009]

Soumah, A. (2007) 'Addressing risks through commodity management', presentation at the AFRACA Agribanks Forum.

Subjally, F. (2009) 'Responses to the trade credit crisis from global trade banks', Standard Charters bank presentation in *Trade Finance in the Context of the Global Financial Crisis Course*, 1–5 June, 2009, World Bank Institute, Washington D.C.

Thomas, C.T. (2007) 'Turning warehouses into credit support entities, vision, obstacles and the way forward, presentation at the Asia International Conference.

Tiffen, P. (2006) 'Challenges of sustainable trade and finance', in R. Quirós (ed.) (2007) *Summary of the Conference: Agricultural Value Chain Finance*, p. 39, FAO and Academia de Centroamérica, San José, available from: www.ruralfinance.org/id/54079 [accessed 24 September 2009]

Torrebiarte, P. (2006) 'Asistencia técnica, mitigación de riesgo y acceso a servicios financieros', presentation at the Latin American Conference.

United Nations Conference on Trade and Development (UNCTAD) Secretariat (2002) 'Farmers and farmers associations in developing countries and their use of modern financial instruments', study prepared by the UNCTAD Secretariat, January 2002.

Vorley, B., Lundy, M. and MacGregor, J. (2008) 'Business models that are inclusive of small farmers', in C. da Silva, D. Baker, A. Shepherd, C. Jenane, and S. Miranda-da-Cruz (eds) (2009) *Agro-industries for development*, FAO, UNIDO, IFAD and CABI.

Wairo, F. (2007) 'FPEAK: Kenya-GAP, addressing quality and safety standards of Kenyan production', presentation at the AFRACA Agribanks Forum.

Wenner, M. (2006) 'Lecciones aprendidas en el financiamiento de las cadenas agrícolas de valor: El caso del BID', presentation at the Latin American Conference.

Winn, M., Miller, C. and Gegenbauer, I. (2009) 'The use of structured finance instruments in agriculture in ECA countries', *AGSF Working Document No. 26*, FAO, Rome.

World Bank (2005) *Rural Finance Innovation Report*, The World Bank, Washington D.C.

World Bank (2008) *World Development Report 2008: Agriculture for Development*, The World Bank, Washington D.C.

World Bank (2009) Doing Business 2009, Washington D.C., [online] www.doingbusiness.org [accessed 24 September 2009]

Wortelboer, H. (2007) 'Rabobank: agri-revolution', presentation at the Asia International Conference.

Zamora, E. (2006) 'Modelo LAFISE: Desarrollo de Alianzas y Financiamiento de la Cadena Productiva y Comercialización', presentation at the Latin American Conference.

Index